BROKEN MARKETS

A USER'S GUIDE TO THE POST-FINANCE ECONOMY

Kevin Mellyn

Apress

Broken Markets: A User's Guide to the Post-Finance Economy

Copyright © 2012 by Kevin Mellyn

ISBN-13 (pbk): 978-1-4302-4221-5

ISBN-13 (electronic): 978-1-4302-4222-2

President and Publisher: Paul Manning
Acquisitions Editor: Jeff Olson
Editorial Board: Steve Anglin, Mark Beckner, Ewan Buckingham, Gary Cornell, Louise Corrigan, Morgan Ertel, Jonathan Gennick, Jonathan Hassell, Robert Hutchinson, , Michelle Lowman, James Markham, Matthew Moodie, Jeff Olson, Jeffrey Pepper, Douglas Pundick, Ben Renow-Clarke, Dominic Shakeshaft, Gwenan Spearing, Matt Wade, Tom Welsh
Coordinating Editor: Rita Fernando
Copy Editor: Damon Larson
Compositor: SPi Global
Indexer: SPi Global
Production Editor: Brigid Duffy
Cover Designer: Anna Ishchenko

Distributed to the book trade worldwide by Springer-Verlag New York, Inc., 233 Spring Street, 6th Floor, New York, NY 10013. Phone 1-800-SPRINGER, fax (201) 348-4505, e-mail orders-ny@springer-sbm.com, or visit www.springeronline.com.

For information on translations, please contact us by e-mail at info@apress.com, or visit www.apress.com.

Apress and friends of ED books may be purchased in bulk for academic, corporate, or promotional use. eBook versions and licenses are also available for most titles. For more information, reference our Special Bulk Sales–eBook Licensing web page at www.apress.com/bulk-sales. To place an order, email your request to support@apress.com

To John Edward Mellyn, Sr.
(4/23/1914–1/16/2011)
DFC 1944

Contents

Foreword

For those of us who still find the reading of books a useful tool in understanding how the world around us works—or doesn't work—the last five years have provided a nearly overwhelming deluge of postmortems on the financial market meltdown that gripped the planet in 2007 and continues in slightly muted fashion to this very day. If you wanted to, you could still be reading them, dawn until dusk, day after day, in search of answers. Nothing gets writers more excited than a crisis, after all.

While they come in many different flavors, the majority of those books share a simple yet frustratingly elusive goal: finding the answer to that most human of questions, *Whose fault was this?* While a focused anger at "fat cat" bankers still runs at a low boil in 2012, the fact of the matter is that there is more than enough blame to go around, with culprits that range from greedy Wall Streeters to ineffective regulators, (arguably) well-intentioned politicians, clueless central bankers, crony capitalism, and, yes, even a reckless and covetous body public. *All the Devils Are Here*, by Bethany McLean and Joe Nocera (Portfolio, 2010), does a fine job at parsing the diffuse "responsibility" for the crisis, if you can call it that.

A handful of books look in another direction and focus on those who emerged from the chaos as "winners"—as unpalatable as such an exercise may seem in the midst of such collective loss. I contributed my own effort to that smaller pile with *Last Man Standing: The Ascent of Jamie Dimon and JPMorgan Chase* (Simon & Schuster, 2010), as did Greg Zuckerman of the *Wall Street Journal*, with *The Greatest Trade Ever* (Crown Business, 2009), about John Paulson's stupendously profitable (and perfectly timed) short trade against the housing bubble. Along with a few self-congratulatory prognosticators who I shall leave unnamed, this smaller cohort sought the answer to the secondary question of *Who saw this coming?*

A third category aimed for what we in the business call tick-tock storytelling—these authors chronicled as best they could just who was doing what, where, and when as the whole house of cards fell in on itself. *Too Big to Fail*, by Andrew Ross Sorkin of the *New York Times* (Viking Adult, 2009), sucked most of the air out of the room on that count; the book was a celebrated success that culminated in HBO's movie by the same name. I'm no expert on the subject, but I am comfortable with my unscientific conclusion that the 2011 movie is quite likely the most watched financial-markets thriller ever to grace the small screen.

What's been missing from the still-growing list of books is the kind of effort that eschews the narrative temptations of either villainy or heroism, and makes a sober attempt to step back and ask the more basic questions of whether this thing was ever really avoidable at all, regardless of which actors got marquee billing for what roles. The answers to those questions—*How did this happen?* and *Why did this happen?*—may not sell as well at the box office or on Amazon.com, but they are arguably the most important ones we should be seeking if we hope to avoid playing out yet another act in Karl Marx's perennially and maddeningly correct dictum that history appears first as tragedy and then returns as farce.

But such a book isn't missing anymore. It has come in the form of Kevin Mellyn's *Broken Markets*, a book that's achieved the remarkable accomplishment of being both refreshingly dispassionate *and* highly readable. I first read it while lying on the beach in the Bahamas, if you can believe that, and not only did it not ruin my vacation, but it allowed me to claim that I'd actually been "working" on more than my tan while I was there.

————

Kevin Mellyn is not your typical business writer.

For starters, he's not even a writer by trade. Or at least he wasn't until recently. He's spent the majority of his professional career as a management consultant and an international banker. And from that, we all benefit. His deep understanding of just *how* banking systems work—and have worked for centuries—encompasses both the small (e.g., payment systems) and the so big as to be nearly ungraspable (e.g., the philosophy of financial repression).

If he came to writing late in the game, though, he's certainly brought with him an arsenal that should strike fear in the heart of anyone working on the topic he sets his sights on next. First and foremost in that arsenal is an utterly obvious love of history. Whether he's riffing on the differences between Bonaparte and his namesake nephew, quoting British marching songs from the American Revolutionary War, or reminding us of the simple yet profound observations of Victorian banker and journalist Walter Bagehot, Mellyn's span of context far exceeds practically every other attempt to put the events of our time in the longer (yet still quite relevant) historical continuum.

He's also brought with him a remarkable restraint of pen, especially considering that this is a man whose opinions come with such force and clarity that it is an ill-advised conversation partner who tries to take him on when the topic is one he's passionate about. Take, for example, political philosophy. Mellyn espouses a certain Victorian liberalism, a bias for personal liberty and the rule of law, and a wholesome fear of power. That's not to say he doesn't know a few of those powerful people himself. (The fact that the man belongs to "clubs" in Boston, New York, and London should serve as proof beyond a reasonable doubt.)

And while he's not the kind of guy who's going to vote for Barack Obama this fall, he isn't going to decide that he's got nothing to say to you if *you* are. In other words, he writes as a conservative that even a liberal Democrat such as myself can learn to love—with scholarship and conviction, yet also enough balance to make it all go down easily enough. Of course, he can't resist the occasional jab at Bill Clinton or Franklin Roosevelt (although it never comes soaked in meanness). Kevin Mellyn is a reasonable man, and he's writing for everyone, not just some partisan slice of the populace looking to glory in its own echo chamber.

Even when it's clear, for example, that he thinks liberals' love of an overprotective state gets us in more trouble than it avoids, he is fair enough to give individual actors the benefit of the doubt about their intentions. Nor does he spare the rod when his intellectual allies deserve it—like most of us, he, too, is flabbergasted by the fact that reform of outrageous Wall Street pay practices has fallen cravenly short of the mark. On that front, the book is a breath of fresh air in a time when the accompanying political vitriol usually comes in extreme disproportion to any important matters at hand.

I won't ruin the plot for you, but in his stated goals—explaining just how the world's financial markets came to be so broken and putting forth a cogent (and seemingly possible) argument for how we might fix them—Mellyn succeeds with aplomb. And he does so while offering an enjoyable smattering of what those of us who know him have come to refer to as Mellynsims—humorous and pithy observations that bring to mind a writer I'm quite sure he's never been compared to in his short career as one: the *New Yorker*'s Hendrik Hertzberg.

In short, *Broken Markets* is a well-argued manifest for a return to first principles in how we all manage our money. And it is one that is made in the aim of the universally acceptable hope that even if we can't entirely avoid busts, we might somehow be able to mitigate their painful effects in the future. If you're like me, you may be thinking that you've already had your fill of books about the recent debacle. In that case, allow me to recommend that you make room for at least one more. Hell, I'd even suggest taking it to the beach.

Duff McDonald

Contributing Editor
Fortune magazine

About the Author

Kevin Mellyn is a management consultant, author, and former international banker residing in Bronxville, New York. He has more than 30 years of experience in almost every aspect of global finance and banking. Mellyn is the author of *Financial Market Meltdown* (Praeger, 2009)—required reading for new recruits in a leading global financial-services firm—a short history and explanation of financial markets, manias, and panics to help the general reader understand and cope with the calamity of 2008. He has been widely published and quoted in financial publications in the U.S., Europe and Asia. Mellyn holds AB and AM degrees in history from Harvard University.

Acknowledgments

This book exists because of three people. First, my editor Jeff Olson of Apress who began last September to prod me to write another book about finance for his new imprint. Jeff had nursed my last effort into print and believed that I had something more to say about the financial world that would interest and benefit the general reader. Since I am anything but a professional author and could not take any time off from my work to actually focus on a book, I was initially very skeptical. His faith in my work won me over, as did the really impressive support and technology his imprint provides to authors. Second, since I am a confirmed technophobe and can't type to save my life, my very clever and talented wife Judy turned my hundreds of sheets of yellow legal pads filled with late night scribbling into polished and proof read pages. Without Judy, neither this nor my last book would have seen print. I especially benefited from her patience with my being absorbed in writing almost every free moment for nearly four months. Books are not easy on spouses in the best of circumstances. I am often grumpy when overtired and under pressure, so I suspect no fun to have under foot. Third, my daughter Elizabeth Mellyn, who really is a scholar and teacher of history, offered great encouragement and good counsel to her amateur dad.

In order to write this type of book, the author needs the help of two kinds of people: teachers and mentors on one hand and constructive critics on the other. As for teacher, my education in finance and banking was an accident of personal history when in 1974 I left academic pursuits to make a living in the "real world," a place for which I was and remain somewhat ill suited. I was lucky to get hired by the International Division of Manufacturers Hanover Trust and even luckier in my first boss and mentor, John Altenau. I spent the late 1970s and early 1980s with MHT in the City of London before it became Americanized. That experience has served me well ever since. It was in London that I first got drawn into a McKinsey project that led to my subsequent transition into management consulting. I cannot name everyone I learned about banking from in those MHT years but Harry Taylor, Fulvio Dobrich, and Sam Newman stand out. Later, as a consultant with the Mitchell Madison Group, I learned a great deal of what is in this book from my clients, especially Patrick Perry, then the Group Treasurer at Barclays. The list could become very long indeed.

As for readers and critics, the electronic publishing process leaves very little time between completing a manuscript and going into production so unavoidably many of the constructive comments of those kind enough to read my chapters are not reflected in the final text. I have tried to incorporate "red flags" where my arguments were running off the road, but for better or worse the errors in this book are mine.

My volunteer readers keep expanding but I would here like to thank author and journalist Duff McDonald, British political commentator Bruce Anderson, Kenneth Cukier of the *Economist*, Arthur Mitchell of White & Case in Tokyo, Takayoshi Hatayama of Abeam Consulting in Tokyo, economists Bernard Connolly and Matthew Saal, payments experts Eric Grover and Michael Lewis, as well as Angus Walker, Antony Elliot of Fairbanking, historian and author Louis Hyman, and Professor Hal Scott, director of the Harvard Law School Program on the International Financial System, legal scholar Fred Kellogg, David Asper of AT Kearney, Rajiv Shah of Deloitte, Andre Cappon of the CBM Group and Pierre Buhler for their interest and input. Many others have offered their encouragement and I hope no offense is taken by anyone I failed to mention.

Finally, writing a book like this over such a short time span would have been beyond my abilities without the helpful but firm support of the Apress staff, especially Rita Fernando.

Introduction

The ability of individuals to access information has never been greater thanks to the internet. In the case of the Financial Market Meltdown of 2008, this has been less than helpful for the intelligent lay reader who just wants to make sense of what has happened and where things might go. A Google search for "financial crisis" yields about 24,000,000 entries, and the crisis has spawned many hundreds of books by journalists, academics, and others. Most of these books have some merit or they would have ended up in the infamous slush heap of proposals and manuscripts where every publisher and book agent consigns the vast majority of submissions. However, since publishing is a business like any other, most of this vast output falls into two categories.

The first, and by far the most successful in terms of sales, is the financial equivalent of a John Grisham legal thriller, only in non-fiction format. The stark reality that Grisham overcame is that law is deadly dull, as is finance, when done correctly. To be exciting, it needs to be made exciting by extreme situations and larger-than-life characters. Above all, the reader needs to feel that there is a dark and sinister cabal of powerful men (the baddies are seldom women) behind events and that the author has, through dogged investigative journalism, unmasked them. The former junior bond trader Michael Lewis perfected this genre in 1989 when the 1987 market crash was on everyone's mind and he indeed managed to make the grotesque realities of Wall Street both funny and alarming. Everything since is derivative to some degree.

The problem with these books overall is that they all arrive at the startling conclusion that very greedy and often stupid people were recklessly rolling the dice at the big Wall Street banks. This is the moral equivalent of Captain Renault saying of Rick's Café in *Casablanca*: "I'm shocked, shocked to find that gambling is going on in here!" The behavior of financial professionals has probably never been too much different than in the era leading up to the crisis, only the balance between fear and greed got seriously out of control as it does on a pretty regular basis over time. No matter what measures are taken by governments, this will no doubt happen again, common human nature being what it is. Besides, there is plenty in the story of the late crisis and indeed the whole historic record to suggest that politicians and regulatory bureaucrats are no better than greedy bankers. They just play for different prizes and like power more than money. Only a few books have cast light of the egregious behavior of politicians from both parties in growing the housing bubble at the epicenter of the meltdown. Again, it is hard to see why any adult would be surprised to find a well-oiled machine connecting the housing industry, politicians, and their paymasters in Washington and Wall Street. The real question is what can or should the average man or woman believe and how they should manage their financial lives? Here the shock-horror financial journalism falls short, entertaining as it often is. I doubt any of these books will be read or in print a year or two from now.

The second category of book involves serious academic research and, at best, the ability to make complex realities simple and interesting. And, unlike the greed-and-corruption literature, they put things in historical context, sometimes centuries. The late Charles Kindleberger was the master in this regard, though for the 2008 crisis *This Time Its Different* by Ken Rogoff and Carmen Reinhart might represent the gold standard. Certainly the events of the last five years will keep both economists and economic historians busy for generations, as the Great Depression of the 1930s continues to stimulate research and controversy. Like the less substantive financial thrillers, these more serious works tend to leave the "so what?" for the common reader less than clear.

The problem with both categories of crisis literature is that they are not, to borrow a term, user friendly. *Broken Markets* is essentially an attempt to connect the dots for the busy non-specialist rather than to break new ground. In fact, it was written entirely from my personal memory and secondary sources since I had neither time nor resources to conduct proper research. This was also true of my earlier book on the crisis, or rather the nature of all financial crises *Financial Market Meltdown* (Praeger, 2009). Both books take their inspiration from the great Victorian banker and journalist Walter Bagehot, creator of the *Economist* newspaper, who wrote in a very similar way since he had two jobs as banker and journalist. Bagehot tried very hard to make abstractions like money and credit concrete and easily understood by educated laymen. In other words, knowing the subject intimately through long experience, Bagehot replaced the mystery of the financial market with plain words and what he called "real history," the explanation of why the arrangements we take for granted like paper money and consumer credit are really just accidents of history that hardened into institutions. Bagehot in other words made finance and writing about it user friendly. This book is my humble attempt to follow his example.

Like Bagehot's classic *Lombard Street* (1873), this book is really a series of essays that can be read independently but work best as a single extended essay on the topic: "What happens to us all once the governments of the world make finance safe?" Essentially, it is an extended conversation about the economic consequences, intended and unintended, of the pendulum of financial regulation swinging too far from market friendly liberalization to an attempt to eliminate the risk of another such crisis at all costs. Like any long conversation, it has a number of digressions intended to fill in background or underline arguments. It is meant to provoke thought rather than provide simple answers for the reader. That is what I mean by the subtitle of the book—a user's guide to the world after finance. If I have succeeded at all, you will end up questioning and drawing your own conclusions about every piece of journalism, political advocacy, or financial advice directed at you from an informed perspective.

This is important because financial crises have complex origins but ultimately rest on simple human frailty. We all want to believe that good times have solid foundations, that things are only getting better, and that we can become prosperous and secure. Optimism is no bad thing, and Americans in particular are prone to it, but long periods of collective optimism in the world of finance leads to ever-rising asset prices, often called manias or bubbles. If these are largely confined to common stock, as was the case during the dot.com mania, a sudden collapse in prices makes a lot of people look silly, some crooked, and many investors less rich. When bubbles infect the market for housing, the single most important asset for the vast majority of households, something far more serious is likely to happen when it blows up, and that is precisely what happened.

The housing bubble effectively destroyed the global financial system as it existed in 2007 and brought the economy to its knees. The great temptation is to indulge in the identification of villains and victims and so conveniently forget that everyone, high and low, in America loved the housing bubble as it was happily inflating and any spoilsport daring to suggest reining it in (and there were more that a few) was at best ignored. Congressman Barney Frank insisted in 2003 on the government sponsored housing finance companies continuing "to roll the dice" on sub-prime mortgages and defeated efforts to tighten regulation. These were the loans that blew up the system but in 2003 they found many defenders. It was the spirit of the times.

Although it is far less satisfying than unmasking the naked ambition, greed, and corruption that are constants of business and politics, the truth of all manias is that they are at bottom " extraordinary popular delusions and the madness of crowds" as Scottish journalist Charles Mackay dubbed them in 1841. They only work when more or less everyone believes the unbelievable. Or to quote that great American philosopher Pogo Possum "We have met the enemy and they are us." Rules and regulation have never prevented a financial crisis and won't stop the next one either. More informed and skeptical common sense by users of the financial system just might.

The Rise and Fall of the Finance-Driven Economy

Where We Are Today

> *Hegel remarks somewhere "all great world-historic facts . . . appear twice"; he forgot to add the first time as tragedy, the second time as farce.*
>
> —Karl Marx, *The Eighteenth Brumaire of Louis Bonaparte* (1852)

"Occupy Wall Street" does not quite seem credible as a revolution that can overthrow capitalism, at least not yet. However, the finance-driven economy that transformed America and the world between the early 1980s and the financial market meltdown appears irretrievably broken. The critical question for our economic and political future is whether or not the broken financial markets of today can be mended, by themselves or by the politicians. If they cannot be, we are likely to see a "world without finance" in our future with profound consequences for workers, savers, investors, and employers ... in a word, all of us.

Some years ago, Queen Elizabeth voiced a question that no doubt occupied many minds: why did nobody in the economics profession see the global financial crisis coming? Of course, more than one professional economist did see disturbing trends in the data, but in general, history is often a better guide to understanding where events might take us. As Harvard historian Niall Ferguson once put it, "Yet a cat may look at a king, and sometimes a historian can challenge an economist."

The lessons of history are constantly being revisited and debated by professional historians. This chapter is not a part of that debate. But even a layman can and should use history, which is after all our common memory as a society, to understand our present and make decisions about our future. So even a layman can thread together a narrative about how the current and continuing crisis will most likely play out.

The current crisis is not the first time the global financial system has effectively collapsed. Fortunately or unfortunately, the world has lived through the rise and fall of a finance-driven economy before. The real question is whether we have learned anything useful from the experience and whether we can avoid repeating the worst outcomes of the original tragedy.

It is somewhat surreal to think of how the leaders of global finance were Masters of the Universe only a few years ago. Today, bankers are demonized, and the very legitimacy and social usefulness of the financial markets and the firms and people that work in them is challenged from every quarter. In fact, "anti-capitalism" has reemerged from the dustbin of history.

Nobody who lived through the Cold War and marveled at the collapse of revolutionary socialism (i.e., communism) as a real-world alternative to capitalist democracy in 1989–1991 ever expected to see so many neo-Marxist slogans brandished by protesters "occupying Wall Street" just over 20 years later. Nor did it seem possible that seas of red flags with a hammer and sickle would flood the streets of Athens and Rome. But not only is the backlash against global finance capitalism very real, it is growing, and more than a few members of the political class and media are hoping it succeeds.

What Karl Can Teach Us

None of us should be surprised that anti-capitalism, even Marxism, is in the air again. Marx never entirely goes away, partially because he remains a great and original observer of how the world really works, including how politics follows economics. His critique of capitalism, a term he more or less defined, may be wrong. But it is not stupid. And he knew how to learn from history.

Marx's world was shaped by two revolutions, one political and one economic. The French Revolution, which destroyed the old order in all of Europe, grew out of a deep economic crisis that was a direct result of France spending too much and borrowing too much, mostly to finance war. To Marx, the tragedy of the French Revolution was that after ten years it was hijacked by Napoleon (the first 18th Brumaire was Bonaparte's seizure of power in 1799). The farce was his nephew Louis Bonaparte's seizure of power 1851, shutting down the far less radical Revolution of 1848. Both men paid lip service to the ideals of the French Revolution, including equality. Both were opportunists who used crises to grab power. But only the original Bonaparte's coup mattered enough to be tragic.

Perceptive as Marx could be about politics, his real project was making sense of the economic revolution that was unfolding before his eyes. This is not so much the so-called industrial revolution we learned about in school (presuming anyone is still taught history), but the rise of global finance capital. His big idea, grossly simplified, was that capital was a force unto itself, and a very destructive one. Basically, capital (today we talk about "wealth") gets concentrated in fewer and fewer hands through market competition, capturing larger and larger portions of income and beggaring labor, the real source of value. Overproduction and speculation lead to ever more severe and frequent economic crises. The capitalist system's contradictions lead to its own demise as the conditions of the masses become intolerable.

A key factor in this process, one that Marx took for granted as a resident of Victorian Britain, was that capital flowed freely around the world, ruthlessly seeking the highest returns. In other words, there was a global financial marketplace that allowed capital to become concentrated into fewer and fewer hands. Of course, today we call integration of markets for goods, services, and money "globalization," and for much of the last decade we have debated whether it was a good thing or a bad thing. Actually, to the Victorians, including Marx, global markets were a fact of life, and barriers to moving capital were almost nonexistent. Between 1815 and 1914, especially in the second half of the period, the combination of a British Empire committed to free trade, the pound sterling backed by gold as anchor currency for the world, and London as the world's money market allowed capital to go anywhere it could make a good return. Contemporaries called this system of free markets and the limited constitutional government that went with it *liberalism*, almost the opposite of how the word is used in America today.

Looking back, in this first great age of globalization, finance capital radiating out of London built the modern industrial world and ushered in the greatest rise in living standards in human history. It also ushered in a very wretched industrial working class. Looking at it up close from Marx's perspective, and he was scarcely alone at the time or since, the old rhythms of agriculture and artisan production were replaced by an icy "cash nexus" where human beings were reduced to lumps of labor for capital to exploit. The gap between rich and poor was becoming intolerable, and financial booms and busts followed by deep downturns in the real economy more frequent and extreme. Surely the revolution would come . . . only it didn't. Instead, the Great Powers, including liberal England, went to war with each other.

The First World War almost put an end to liberal order and the first great age of global finance capital, but its immediate effect was to kill off the reactionary empires of Europe, Russia, Austria-Hungary, Germany, and Turkey. Revolution, where it did come, was the product of military defeat, not the revolt of "the 99 percent." The great goal of the war's victors, especially the United States, who got in late and came out rich and powerful, was to get back to what Warren Harding famously called "normalcy." It seemed obvious that the global financial system that had been in place before the war could and should be put back together. This meant that countries that had moved off the gold standard during the conflict would get back on it as quickly as possible, and that means would be found to work off the mountains of government debt the war had generated. The big difference was that it was New York, not London, that held the keys of the global financial system. Having been a destination of global finance capital for a century, America became the world's creditor as well as the biggest industrial economy. For a while it worked: global capital flows were eventually rejiggered, so the Americans loaned money to the Germans so the Germans could pay enough in reparations to the French and British to service the huge sums they had borrowed in New York during the war. Of course, nobody was really paying what was owed, but a booming Wall Street kept the money flowing.

And Wall Street did boom, partially in response to pro-business policies in Washington, but mainly in response to a whole wave of new technologies being transformed into mass consumption goods such as automobiles and radios. A new type of credit, consumer finance, emerged to make the new goods affordable. Stocks seemed to only go in one direction, up. So did paper wealth, at least among those fortunate enough to have the money to play the market. Real estate prices followed stocks up. America was awash in money.

Beneath the Wall Street froth, however, all was not well on Main Street. Leveraging new technologies and methods of doing work, such as the assembly line, industrial productivity (the hours of labor needed to produce something) was outstripping wages and purchasing power. Farms and small-town banks failed in droves during the Roaring Twenties. Few noticed, but the economy was being driven by an "asset bubble" in common stocks inflated by easy money, especially loans to purchase shares—so-called margin credit—and unbounded optimism.

A boom, or bubble, economy supported by borrowing against inflated assets can be sustained for long periods as long as everyone believes prices will continue to rise. The dot-com bubble of the 1990s was a classic case of this. To be fair, at least the stock market darlings of the 1920s were real companies, such as RCA and Studebaker, making real products and real profits.

Financial history tells us that all bubbles end in busts, often very nasty ones, but these are usually limited to one country and only rarely compromise the global economy. Even the catastrophic bursting of the Japanese bubble economy in 1989, despite its lingering effects even now after 20 years, had very limited consequences for global markets.

What made the bursting of the Wall Street bubble in October of 1929 and the events that followed unique was not just the depth and duration of the economic pain in the United States, but that the market collapse was global in scope. The events of the 1930s are a source of endless fascination and controversy because so many narratives can be constructed around its causes and effects.

Wall Street had seen dramatic busts before, such as the Panic of 1907, but they were neither global nor long lasting in their consequences. In 1929, however, the initial market crash was followed by an avalanche of disasters, many of them self-inflicted by policy makers, which effectively destroyed the liberal order and the global financial system that made it work. The Great Depression not only set the stage for a global war of unparalleled destructiveness, but it vastly expanded the role and power of government in shaping the economy and society itself—a profound break with the classical liberal tradition.

Are we about to repeat the trauma of the Great Depression? We have much better analytical and policy tools at our disposal today than were available in the 1930s, plus the great advantage of having lessons of what went wrong in the 1930s to guide us. Moreover, the world was still mending from a devastating general war in 1929 and was far, far poorer than it is today. This does not mean, however, that we should dismiss the idea of a replay.

The Current Movie

History never quite repeats itself, but, as Mark Twain paraphrased Marx, it does rhyme. We can think through our investment, public policy, and business strategy options (we always have options, even when they are all bad) by understanding the "movie" or narrative of how financial crises unfold and how things turn out in the final reel. Besides the Great Depression, we have the benefit of several smaller B movies—banking implosions limited to one country. (The biggest headliner is the Japanese financial crisis of the 1990s.) Finally, we have the most recent version, the financial market meltdown of 2008, though the shooting is not yet complete.

The plot summary goes like this.

Scene One

Low interest rates and easy money encourage overinvestment and speculation that gradually builds into a boom or mania. Usually this is led by one investment type or *asset class*, such as common stock in the 1920s. But as optimism spreads through the economy, all asset prices go up. There are no bad investments in a boom. There are also very few bad loans or deals that cannot get done, so the financial sector does very, very well compared to other industries, and the share of wealth and income captured by bankers explodes.

Scene Two

An event—often a key bank revealing unexpected weakness or a central bank raising rates to "cool" overexuberence—causes a sudden break in the upward trajectory of asset prices, or they simply stop rising due to overinvestment, just as US house prices did in 2006. This breaks the spell of universal optimism and makes markets, especially overnight interbank funding markets, nervous about which financial institutions are holding bad assets.

Scene Three

Every major financial center revolves around a "money market" where, in normal market conditions, banks with surplus deposits lend them to other banks that are short funds overnight and for longer terms. In scene three, such interbank lending dries up and interbank loan spreads spike as institutions try to protect themselves from each other. Banks hoard their surplus funds (those that they have no immediate need of) in central banks such as the European Central Bank (ECB) and the US Federal Reserve in a rush toward safety and liquidity. Asset prices tumble as credit required to finance investment activity evaporates.

Scene Four

As the flow of bank credit to households and businesses dries up, the "authorities" (central banks and national treasuries) try to pump liquidity into the money market. (Any country that issues a currency can create infinite amounts of it through its central bank. This is also known as "printing money.") Pumping money into the market also drives down its price (in other words, interest rates). This part of the plot was not really tried in the 1930s version, and often blamed for the worst of the slump. Since the 1940s it has become part of almost every remake.

Scene Five

If it looks like banks are going to fall over like dominos, central banks and treasuries will resort to making asset purchases and even direct capital injections into the banks. Shotgun weddings putting weak or walking-dead banks together into larger players are encouraged or compelled. Once this could be done with private capital, as when J. P. Morgan singlehandedly stopped the Panic of 1907. Now the banking sector is so large and interwoven that many individual banks are "too big to fail," which in practice means the government (i.e., the taxpayers) has to save them from collapse. Although so-called bailouts are politically toxic, not doing them risks total economic collapse. Thus, sooner or later, they get into the story line.

Scene Six

More subtly, the authorities try to restore banks to profitability so they can go back to lending to businesses and households. The easiest way to do this is by providing essentially free money to the banks so they can "earn" a spread on government bonds, or even by hoarding money at the central bank. These artificially created bank earnings are meant to rebuild confidence and stability in the financial markets and a restoration of "normal" credit conditions.

Scene Seven

In this scene, nothing that is supposed to happen actually does. First, there is limited demand for borrowing in the real economy, the actual exchange of goods and services, which remains in shock from the destruction of wealth caused by the collapse of asset prices (over $13 trillion was wiped off the balance sheet of the US household sector during 2008–2009). Anybody who actually needs money faces a credit crunch caused by the restoration of prudent (or hyper-prudent) lending standards. Banks are terrified of lending into a falling economy.

Scene Eight

Regulation is greatly expanded and tightened, setting off more adverse consequences on credit availability. Banks become political and legal targets of opportunity. The 1933 Pecora hearings in Congress featured the ritual humiliation of J. P. Morgan himself, but the Banking Act of 1933 (aka the Glass-Steagall Act which barred banks from the investment business) was based on a vaguely coherent view that bank fed speculation led to the Crash of 1929. The Dodd-Frank act, which was jammed through Congress before the completion of a congressional report, was arguably more a compromise between long-held political objectives, such as enhanced regulation of consumer financial services, and pushback by lobbyists than an attempt to address root causes like excessive extension of credit to consumers (more on this in Chapter 2).

Scene Nine

Sovereign debt vastly increases due to financial sector bailouts and depressed tax receipts from the shrinking real economy, rising unemployment, and associated social safety net spending. States with weak public finances lose debt market access and veer toward default (with Greece being the poster boy this time around). Meanwhile, regulatory capital rules—as well as risk aversion to the real economy and lack of loan demand by shell-shocked enterprises and households—have stuffed bank balance sheets with sovereign bonds. Central bank balance sheets are whole multiples of pre-crisis levels due to bad asset purchases and "quantitative easing"—central banks creating money to buy debt securities.

Scene Ten

The finance crisis seems contained, and states and banks hope for a return to something resembling pre-crisis conditions or recovery while they continue to patch over difficulties ad hoc (e.g., Greece, Ireland, US house prices). Recovery in the real economy and meaningful reductions in unemployment remain elusive. Markets swing wildly from hope (risk-on) to fear (risk-off) on political or corporate-earnings news.

Scene Eleven

An unanticipated shock delivers the system a blow that it has no remaining resources, tools, or will to withstand. The financial system collapses for a second time to the point that it has to be restarted more or less from scratch under new rules, with most of the power being transferred from the markets to the state that provided the resources, essentially a far more radical version of what happened in the US after the Bank Holiday of 1933.

Scene Twelve

The aftermath of financial crisis rarely leads to the state simply recapitalizing the banks and exiting the business, though something very like this happened in Sweden in the 1990s. Most often, crises are followed by the systematic imposition of "financial repression"—a regime in which the state systematically suppresses market forces in finance—especially interest rates—in order to direct credit for political ends and hold down its own funding costs. This regime leaves itself open to democratic crony capitalism at best. At worst, it leads to socialism or "corporatism"—the organization of society into collective interest groups such as big business and labor, all subordinate to the state (as with Italy and Germany and even some aspects of the New Deal). Financial repression is how banking works in China today, and once in place, it is very hard to change.

The Banking Act of 1933 ushered in an age of financial repression (and so-called utility banking) in the United States that lasted almost 40 years, until the rise of the euromarkets in London during the 1960s and 1970s allowed US banks and their corporate customers to create a parallel unregulated dollar market outside of US jurisdiction. The much-maligned deregulation of US financial markets only took place much later (the final demise of Glass-Steagall took place on President Bill Clinton's watch), after the repression was no longer effective. And deregulation has proved remarkably easy to throw into reverse. The Dodd-Frank Act, the new Basel III international bank capital regime, and the policies of the European Central Bank make up the new financial repression regime on the hoof, a regime that will likely last for a generation or two. The result will be far slower growth than the finance-driven economy produced from 1983 to 2007. The impact of this will be felt globally because fast-growing export economies and commodity producers in developing markets rely on growth and consumption in the developed economies. There is far less decoupling of the fates of individual countries in a global economy than is often thought or hoped. The ability to offset depressed US and European growth with emerging market dynamism will likely prove a delusion.

Final Scene and Fade to Credits

Global financial markets will not long remain broken and dormant, as human ingenuity and the desire to make money will always find new ways to connect borrowers and investors. The entrenched, too-big-to-fail institutions left standing by the second leg of the crisis, as well as the most heavily regulated financial centers, will increasingly be bypassed as capital, talent, and customers go elsewhere. Money, like water, always finds a way around efforts to dam it. Innovation trumps regulation over time. In the final scene, global finance reinvents itself in unregulated spaces in developed countries and the dynamic markets of East Asia and beyond. Gradually, the dead hand of the state gives way, and the global financial markets regain their freedom . . . again driving rapid economic growth, until the next catastrophic financial bubble that nobody saw building up explodes.

Where We Are Now

We are teetering on the cusp of scenes ten and eleven. We might still avoid the final tragedy through skill (or dumb luck). We are not passive actors in this movie, and it doesn't have to end in tragedy if we understand where we are in plot and what options are still available to us.

And we must not forget that the market collapse of the 1930s led directly to political tragedy and a global war that killed at least 50 million human beings and that nearly destroyed civilization. Compared to this, the loss of the liberal economic order and the gold standard of the 1920s were small potatoes. The current financial crisis, with any luck, will only destroy the delusions that laws and regulation can make finance safe, but will leave the foundations of economic growth and social stability untouched. We can still reasonably hope that the second great global financial crisis is more farce than tragedy.

The Magic and Poison of Financial Leverage

The size of the financial system relative to the real economy ought to be pretty constant over time, because money is basically just something we use as a convenience or shorthand in exchanging what we have (time, labor, goods, property) for what we want (production, other goods, leisure, status).

Capitalism is not really an ideology, much less a system. At most it describes what happens when the prices of what we have and what we want are set by market bargain, not by custom or authority. The problem is that market bargains are never perfect, much less fair, because the two parties in the transaction are rarely equal in knowledge and power. People make as many bad decisions as good, so the clever and lucky end up with more than their "fair" share of the fruits of production and more money than they have immediate need for.

The financial economy is where this extra money, savings, and investment derived from the real economy gets stored and put to work making more money. Usually this is a benign activity. For example, when a banker gives me a loan for six months so I can plant, harvest, and sell a crop, he is essentially giving me the stuff I need today (tools, labor, seed) to make the money to pay him back tomorrow. The same works for manufacturing and most other forms of commerce. It is called *working capital*, and when it is in short supply, the whole economy grinds to snail's pace. This is why countries without working financial systems (and they are the vast majority) have trouble growing their economies.

The Disconnection Problem

The problems that led to our current unhappy state arise when the financial economy becomes disconnected from the real economy. When that happens, the stocks of financial assets, which are just claims on someone's future production, come to be much larger than the production itself. For example, before the current crisis, the total stock of financial assets, debt, and equity in the United States was $84.3 trillion (year-end 2007) while GDP, the most common measure of production, was only $14 trillion. For the United Kingdom, where the totals are distorted by the activity of non-British firms, the balance sheet of the banking system was five times the size of the real economy.

This disparity between the financial economy and the real economy is stark enough measured as a stock or lump sum of claims. Trading in financial assets dwarfs the real economy's annual turnover by a degree that defies comprehension. Remember, GDP is only a snapshot of final output, so the first sale of a new car gets into the GDP total, but subsequent sale of the same car and many supplier transactions do not. As a result, central bank data compiled by the Bank for International Settlements shows that it took about $500 trillion in real economy payment transactions in 2010 to produce a global GDP of only around $65 to $70 trillion. $500 trillion sounds like a huge number until you compare it with the turnover in purely financial assets traded among banks and other market players around the world, 24 hours a day. Interbank payments settled in the United States alone (around one-third of the global total) amounted to $1,157 trillion in 2007, equities in US depository accounts turned over to the tune of $210 trillion, and US bond transactions came to $671 trillion.

The largest single source of interbank payments is foreign exchange trading. While obtaining foreign exchange is necessary for persons and firms engaged cross-border business and travel, such transactions are a small percentage of turnover, perhaps as little as 1 percent. What accounts for the other $1,000 trillion? The answer is called *professional* or *proprietary trading* if you are a banker, but raw speculation or gambling if you are almost anyone else.

Going back to our movie, remember that this vast disparity between the financial economy and the real economy is essentially new—a product of financial innovation on one hand and the severing of the last constraints on money creation on the other. The 1920s bubble economy was based on stock prices vastly outpacing any realistic future productions and profits by the companies involved. These inflated stock price values were multiplied by excessive borrowing against them, both for speculative purchase of more stock on credit (so-called margin loans by stock brokers) and for consumption and real estate investment. Another word for this disparity is *leverage*. As long as the banking system is *solvent*—that is, it can continue to make loans—leverage is pure magic. Essentially, it means more economic activity takes place and more wealth gets generated. If I have to finance expansion of my business out of retained profits, it might take me years to do so. If a bank gives me the money, I can do it immediately. The same goes for a consumer buying a car or major appliance—access to borrowed money makes it happen sooner and often at higher sticker prices. A finance-driven economy, managed prudently, is a dynamic economy.

The problem arises when financial leverage outstrips the ability of firms and households to generate income (or worse, becomes a substitute for income). This is very much what happened in the US domestic economy between the 1980s and the market meltdown of 2008. Leverage helped America create jobs and economic growth at a pace that more financially conservative Europe could not match. But what looked like magic in the rosy days of the Clinton boom was actually a mounting level of poison in the economic bloodstream. Essentially, leverage became a substitute for real income growth among the vast majority of Americans. At the same time, the United States became, to an extraordinary degree, dependent on consumer spending rather than production. Over a 20-year period, consumer debt went from about half of household assets to over 120 percent. In addition, real inflation-adjusted wages stagnated or fell, as almost all income gains flowed to holders of financial assets.

The Financialization of Wealth

This "financialization" of wealth is not entirely new. The finance capital Marx focused on was much the same in principle. So was the wealth that concentrated itself in the hands of common-stock owners in the Roaring Twenties. What was new was its sheer scale and its sources. The financialized wealth of the 1982–2007 boom was concentrated in two types of people: the beneficiaries of stock-based compensation granted by public companies—itself a result of efforts to curb the cash compensation of executives—and participants in the financial services industry itself, especially investment bankers. This wealth, unlike the finance capital of Marx's day that built the industries of America and railroads around the world, got recycled into more financial trading and risk taking to an extraordinary extent. Partners' funds accumulated in investment banks fed ever more sophisticated proprietary trading operations. Hedge funds—essentially private investment clubs betting on the skills or connections of a stock manager—became real forces in the capital markets. Even conservative long-term investors such as pension funds, insurance companies, and university endowments put money into these vehicles, despite the utter lack of transparency and the high fees charged by their managers at the height of the bubble. The share of corporate profits—which of course excludes the hedge funds—generated by the financial services industry (broadly defined) hit 22 percent.

The key to this was less genius than it was leverage. Investment banks, once partnerships trading on their own capital, became public companies. They used the capital raised in the market to increase their leverage by issuing debt. Hedge funds became some of the largest borrowers from the leading commercial banks. The game only worked if the value of financial assets and companies kept going up.

Two things were necessary to make this happen. First, companies themselves had to bend all their efforts to meet the quarterly profit expectations of the professional investors. This meant that, unless they were so-called growth stocks in new technologies, they needed to cut costs relentlessly where and when so-called top-line growth failed to meet profit targets. The burden of this fell directly on labor, which because of the emergence of technology-driven breakthroughs in efficiency and companies' ability to source low-cost production and services in China, India, and other emerging markets found itself competing with what Marx called "the reserve army of labor" on a global basis. Outrage over "shipping jobs overseas,"—aka *outsourcing*—was of no practical benefit, because low-cost labor was of less significance than investment in productivity-enhancing technologies. Productivity gains over the long run tend to raise living standards, but a very large share of these gains was captured in corporate profits and by workers overseas.

Second, corporate profits themselves could be manipulated by management. Stock-based compensation was intended to align the interests of the owners of a company, the shareholders, with those of executive management. When the company did well, management did well, because the stock price should rise and reward both. This was a neat solution to the so-called agency problem, in which the interest of the hired help (as JP Morgan explicitly viewed the executives of companies he owned) and the owners conflict. In practice, managers know all the ins and outs of a company, and through timing expenditures and the recognition of losses can to a degree manufacture the quarterly numbers the stock market wants to see. Owners have no such insight, even when boards of directors are not hand-picked by top management, which is usually the case.

Since the basic yardstick of a public company's performance is return on equity, leverage—that is, replacing equity with borrowed money—is a simple means of boosting stock price. So is returning capital directly to the shareholders by buying back stock. Expense reductions, whether by reengineering to eliminate jobs, outsourcing to low-wage markets, or ending so-called defined-benefit pension plans and other benefits, are also levers management can push to increase profits. So-called top-line growth—that is, actually selling more goods and services—is a lot tougher, especially in a mature economy like the United States. However, top-line growth can be bought by acquiring other public companies, keeping most of their customers and revenue, and getting rid of as many costs (and jobs) as possible. The ability to borrow large sums of money—again, leverage—was central to the ability of many "serial acquirers" to grow profits in this way. The mergers-and-acquisitions game also brought enormous fees to the investment banks who negotiated the deals, adding to the concentration of income in the financial industry.

The Rise of the CEO Class

The net result of all these developments was the largest transfer of wealth in history to what we might call the CEO class. This new class is not like the much maligned "robber barons" who actually built whole industries and created million of jobs. A few entrepreneurial heroes stand out—above all, the sainted Steve Jobs—but the CEO class is mainly a technocratic elite of professional managers of established public companies. Its ability to capture as much as a fifth of total corporate profits is a matter of positional power and the tolerance of the institutions that hold their shares.

If, then, most of the increase in American incomes (and wealth, which is harder to measure) was captured by 1 percent of the top 1 percent of earners over the last 25 years, what was the fate of everybody else? The relative income position of the "1 percent" that Occupy Wall Street complains about is distorted by the CEO class and their financiers. The income spread between CEOs and other top executives (the so-called C-Suite, since their titles all seem to start with "Chief") on one hand and line management on the other exploded. Once it was common for a bank's senior vice president or a division head in a company to make a sizable fraction of what the top boss got paid—say $100,000 as opposed to $1,000,000. Now the C-suite and line management live on different planets. Business executives, lawyers, physicians, and other professionals no longer belong to a single broad socioeconomic class, as they had for generations.

For the broad working class that American politicians persist in calling the middle class, things got dramatically worse. Their real incomes have been stagnant or falling for a generation, and whole communities have been stripped of places of employment. Marx would have predicted that the working class would revolt against the CEO class if only out of desperation at their financial predicament. But the remarkable thing, much to the befuddlement of many academic and media observers, is that the middle class became more conservative. Indeed, the union movement—traditional vehicles for workers to push back against capital—has largely collapsed over the last generation. Most union members today are in the public sector. The reasons behind this are complex and controversial but, yet again, financial leverage played a role.

Role of Consumer Debt

The same financial markets that facilitated the financialization of wealth and the rise of the CEO class also managed to turn consumer debt into a viable substitute for income. As historian Louis Hyman points out in *Debtor Nation* (Princeton University Press, 2011), the United States virtually invented consumer credit, and it has profound effects on our economy, politics, and culture. Hyman finds these effects disturbing on many levels, but the fact remains that after World War II the United States became the first country in history to create a dynamic consumer-driven economy on borrowed money. I briefly discuss the mechanics of this in Chapter 2 of this book and in my other book, *Financial Market Meltdown* (Praeger, 2009), though I would urge you to delve into *Debtor Nation* or Hyman's *Borrow* (Random House, 2012) for a fuller critique of the American debt culture and its consequences. The point is that for good or ill, American households were able to continue spending in the face of falling real incomes and negative savings for nearly a generation. As long as consumer debt could be transformed into securities by the Wall Street leverage machine, and Wall Street could sell those securities to institutional investors, including the Chinese, Americans could continue to consume well beyond their earning power. The consumer banking industry would provide households spending money with little or no regard for their ability to repay. Some of this, about $1 trillion, was unsecured revolving credit, mostly provided by a small group of commercial banks.

However, the main driver of consumer debt was $10.5 trillion in mortgage credit, mostly government guaranteed, that allowed nearly 70 percent of US households to "own" a home by 2007. The last few point gains in home ownership was accomplished by a material loosening of lending practices that placed millions of marginal borrowers in houses in which they had made almost no up-front investment and could only afford through loans featuring low "teaser rates." This was partially a product of politics—home ownership for everyone, regardless of means, had appeal to both major parties—and of the Wall Street leverage machine, where mortgage-backed securities drove an inordinate amount of activity and profits. When consumers maxed out their credit cards, they could pay off the balance through refinancing those homes because, of course, house prices only moved in one direction: up. They could take out "excess" equity through so-called HELOCs (home equity lines of credit). People's homes became their ATM, their savings account, and even their pension plan as long as house prices went up and refinancing was easy. The question is not so much why this all came tumbling down in 2008 as it is, "How did this house of cards stay up so long"? The short answer is cheap money over a long period of time.

The Great Moderation

The term *Great Moderation* was coined to describe the 25 years between 1983 and 2008 when inflation remained in check, the value of financial assets rose, and free market capitalism was in the ascendant position it had not occupied since the 1920s. Of course, unless you were sad to see the demise of Marxist-inspired state socialism, times were good with the exception of a few short recessions and a few special cases like Japan. It would be wrong, however, to attribute the Great Moderation to the inherent virtues of a finance-driven global economy where the market rewarded good investments and punished bad ones. For example, the taming of inflation was an heroic one-off accomplishment of Paul Volcker at the Federal Reserve. However, the market reforms during this period in China, and later India, coupled with much improved communications and logistics, greatly expanded the global labor market and lowered the cost of goods that everyday Americans bought. This was no substitute for good central banking, but it certainly made it easier to hold inflation in check. As Asian exports to the United States exploded in volume, the dollar earnings of China and the rest got invested in United States government bonds, including those of the government-sponsored enterprises (GSEs) Fannie Mae and Freddie Mac, which both guaranteed trillions of dollars in consumer mortgages but bought huge amounts of securitized mortgages. These purchases held down interest rates, making consumer debt more affordable. This allowed China, of course, to export more stuff and buy more bonds. Low and stable long-term interest rates allowed housing prices to rise and more people to afford houses.

None of this was due to the genius of policymakers, though a reputed "maestro," Alan Greenspan, occupied the chairmanship of the Board of Governors of the Federal Reserve System for 17 of the 25 years of the Great Moderation. Where the central bank and US Treasury policy was decisive during the Great Moderation was in protecting the financial economy from its own mistakes and excesses. On one level, this made sense, because the sheer scale of the financial economy relative to the real economy made the consequences of a market panic too scary to contemplate in terms of damage to real output and production.

More controversially, the argument can be made that the financialization of wealth had created a new relationship between finance and government. Financial wealth was not reactionary or conservative wealth, but just as likely to be progressive in character. Both Tony Blair's New Labour Party and the Democratic Party under both Bill Clinton and Barack Obama enjoyed the political largesse of financialized wealth, more so than their Tory or Republican opponents. It is no surprise that using the resources of the US Treasury to pull Goldman Sachs's fat out of fire seemed the simple pursuit of national interest. The markets and the largest investment-banking operations increasingly came to believe that the authorities would step in to prevent any reckoning for financial bets gone wrong. In this sense, the Great Moderation was at least as much a product of governments as it was of markets, something that pains the heart of free-market fundamentalists.

The problem is that in a free market, everyone is free to fail. Indeed, something that Joseph Schumpeter called "creative destruction" is essential to economic progress. The Great Moderation was largely a one-way bet for market participants. Financial crises of one sort or another, which affected companies ranging from Japanese and Swedish banks to Long Term Capital, an American hedge fund, continued to occur. In fact, they became more frequent. However, the US Federal Reserve and Treasury were always quick to flood the market with money and slash interest rates in order to limit the damage to the financial economy. Except for the collapse of the dot-com stock market bubble, large-scale destruction of financialized wealth was a thing of the past.

Another problem, of course, is that markets are reflections of human nature, balanced on a knife's edge between fear and greed. To remove fear is to open the floodgates of greed. The problem with greed, whatever the Occupy Wall Street gang might think, is not that it is bad. There is bad and greed in all of us. The problem with greed is that it is careless and often delusional. Fear, specifically fear of losing everything, has always been a healthy antidote to excessive optimism and greed. This is why, in real market capitalism, failure is allowed and even panics have their uses. They purge excess from the system and foster prudence. Individuals and institutions learn from their losses. During the Great Moderation, individuals and institutions learned that the market was back-stopped by the state, their profits were theirs to keep, and their losses would be picked up by the taxpayer.

The Great Panic: Cause and Effect

Much 20/20 hindsight lavished on the financial market meltdown revolves around the collapse of Lehman Brothers and the market freefall that ensued. What made the event so shocking was that the Great Moderation had taught the global financial economy that a large market player with huge obligations to and from other key players would somehow be saved. Certainly Lehman's management must have made this assumption. After all, Bear Stearns, a far less important house with more to answer for in the mortgage securities bubble, had been rescued. Surely, the authorities could see the domino effect that would occur if they let Lehman go down?

Economists use the term *moral hazard* to describe what happens when the consequences of bad decisions are eliminated. For example, deposit insurance means you don't have to evaluate the soundness of your bank. Uncle Sam will always make you whole if it goes bust. What would happen if deposit insurance was abolished overnight during a market panic? There would be a run on the banks as people rushed to turn their deposits into cash before the cash ran out. The failure of one bank would accelerate the failure of others, and soon there would be no banking system aside from the institutions visibly propped up by government.

The deeper causes of the 2008 Great Panic are rehashed in a vast output of books, including my own effort, but the practical effect of letting Lehman fail was to place every institution in the global financial economy in the position of an uninsured depositor to every other institution. Banks that once lent excess funds freely to one another suddenly trusted nobody except central banks. The whole global credit market seized up as banks were reluctant to do much with the funds that central banks were pumping into the system beyond buying government bonds and building up cash in their reserve accounts at the central banks. I'll discuss how regulators and financial uncertainty, especially in Europe, have made this worse, in Chapter 2. The practical effect of a Great Panic was to throw a wrench into the great Wall Street leverage machine.

The Agony of the Household Sector

Up to 2008, with no significant financial wealth, debts in excess of their income—which was in any case stagnant—and diminished employment security, the great American "middle class" continued to drive the economy. Up until 2008, personal consumption accounted for 70 percent of US GDP. The largest positive item on the US household balance sheet was the value of residential property, and the largest negative item was mortgage debt. As long as house prices rose faster than consumer debt, household spending would continue to grow. But that depended on the great Wall Street leverage machine continuing to turn consumer credit into investments. When it became clear that it had gone too far and the machine seized up, so did demand for houses, and therefore their prices fell, especially in the most overheated and overbuilt real estate markets, such as California, Nevada, and Florida.

Since homeowners had been aggressively extracting equity from their houses (in other words, borrowing the difference between the appraised value of the house and the nominal amount owed on the mortgage) for years and many had purchased homes at the top of the bubble, often with little or no down payment, a correction in house prices spelled catastrophe for millions. The net worth of households fell by $7 trillion between 2008 and 2009, excluding gyrations in the price of financial assets. That is the equivalent of all wages and salaries for an entire year simply disappearing. Millions of households—more than one in five mortgage borrowers—woke up to find their houses worth less than the face value of their loans. Since the house-price escalator was the savings retirement plan for the broad middle class—indeed, their only route to financial security—the reality of falling prices was almost impossible to accept. Consumers began to stop paying underwater mortgages and walk away from their houses, sending the keys to the bank in so-called jingle-mail. The stigma of defaulting on a mortgage became replaced with a sense of victimization. The time-honored truism that consumers in difficulty would always pay their mortgage first and their credit card last was turned on its head. Households needed credit cards to buy everyday necessities like gas.

After a generation of debt-fueled consumption, households began to cut back their spending in 2009, and the savings rate turned positive. Household debt levels, having more than doubled in a decade, began to reverse themselves in a process called deleveraging, though much of the reduction in household debt was really due to banks writing off loans as uncollectable. In early 2012, there was actually an uptick in consumer credit, which remains at troubling levels. Putting the household balance sheet on a sustainable footing looks to be a long and bumpy road.

Corporate America Chugs Ahead

Unlike households, American businesses had pretty strong balance sheets going into the market meltdown. A generation of escalating global competition and unforgiving financial markets had taught them how to do more with less and adjust swiftly to changes in demand. Moreover, the largest American corporations were getting ever-larger shares of their sales and profits from the fast-growing emerging markets. They were also basing more of their production and development in places like China, India, and Brazil, which were relatively insulated from the collapse of the US housing bubble. As a result, US industry could react to a crisis in the banking system and consumer confidence by swiftly shedding costs, especially employees, while actually increasing output. Unlike the companies during the crisis of the 1930s, in which profits and employment in large companies fell in tandem, this generation's US companies overall met or exceeded expected earnings in the wake of the initial stock market swoon set off by Lehman's collapse. But they kept their powder dry, hoarding cash and cutting costs where possible.

The real hammer-blow to employment came from the construction industry, which alone accounts for 10 percent of jobs in the US, and businesses dependent on domestic consumer spending, such as retailers and car dealers. Small businesses especially found that banks were no longer willing to lend to them. These sectors also shed jobs, many of them for low-skilled, low-income workers. As such, one of the key predictors of unemployment became educational attainment.

A key vulnerability of a finance-driven economy is that the leverage machine is every bit as powerful when thrown into reverse as it is in forward gear. Spiking unemployment drives defaults on mortgages and credit cards, harming the balance sheets and income statement of the banks, causing them to tighten credit standards, which reduces the ability of consumers to spend on houses and products. This in turn leads to more layoffs and business failure, and hence more unemployment.

The End of Employment

The notion that people have a reasonable expectation of a steady job, usually with hourly pay or salary plus non-cash benefits, is deeply entrenched in our thinking. In our political discourse, there is a central (yet factually unfounded) notion that "creating jobs" is a function of government, or that rich people are somehow "job creators."

The harsh truth of the matter is that the very notion of employment—and its opposite, unemployment—is a product of the rise of big public companies around 1890 or so. Before that, labor was mostly casual, and hands were hired by the day or even the shift. By their very nature, big public companies are essentially bureaucracies, not much different than government bureaus, and are mainly concerned with coordinating activities and resources, including labor. Modern war gave rise to bureaucratic government in the 18th century, and for generations, government service—whether civil or military—was the only full-time employment. Everyone else was self-employed or a hired hand. The reason big public companies like industrial firms and railroads followed the state bureaucratic model was that they needed reliable workers for complicated processes, such as running an automobile assembly line or driving a train. It was more efficient to contract with full-time employees than to fund the workers required as the need arose. Eventually, workers organized into unions that negotiated contracts covering all the workers in a company or industry. This system reached its peak in the 1950s when big business, big labor, and as a referee, big government, presided over what was still an industrial economy.

This system of employment began to fall apart in the 1980s, less than a century after it began, and all the current crisis is really doing is speeding up the process that I call *the end of employment*. Less and less of the economy is engaged in manufacturing, and more is concentrated in services and self-employment. Manufacturing itself has become globalized, so jobs can be readily relocated because of cost or skill factors. Above all, outsourcing and temporary employment have become organized, increasingly efficient markets that provide cheaper ways to contract than the old model of employment.

The finance-driven economy influenced these developments in two important ways. First, financial markets demanded relentless growth in profits, which effectively forced corporations to minimize high-cost, full-time employment in high-wage countries. Second, the buoyant capital markets of the Great Moderation, ever hungry for the next big thing, brought a remarkable number of startup companies to market (Microsoft, Google, Apple, Starbucks, etc.). The ability of a small enterprise to create jobs is limited until it gets the financing to gain scale and grow rapidly. The 1990s capital markets were almost unique in their ability to launch new companies into a growth phase.

The reason we have a jobs crisis, as the chattering class unanimously agrees is the crux of the next election, is not that large, mature firms are not hiring. They rarely do, given global competition. It is that we have ceased to create new enterprises and grow them aggressively.

No Safe Havens

Compounding our problem is the fact that the *investor class*—the minority of the population with stock portfolios of any size—has become traumatized by the events of 2008 and has largely fled the market or gone into wait-and-see mode. That leaves only professional investors, institutional fund managers, and hedge funds, that have to be in the market. The whole market shifts to risk-on when it seems safe to buy equities, and then gallops over to risk-off when equities seem overbought. Sovereign debt (government bonds) used to be safe harbor, but with the euro zone in chronic debt crisis and the United States downgraded on its inability to address its runaway deficit spending, even that refuge seems questionable.

The markets truly are broken. In the following two chapters I will drill down on two key issues that are widely misunderstood by both commentators and the general public. Chapter 2 explains why banking lost its way and became (and in crucial respects remains) dangerous to the general economy, and how many steps taken in the wake of the crisis not only fail to address the core problems but add to them in unintended ways. Chapter 3 spells out the real-life impact of these unintended consequences on the real economy and the man in the street.

Banking, Regulation, and Financial Crises

What Went Wrong with Banking and Why

As human beings, we tend to understand the world around us through stories, or, to use a more formal term, narratives. Without these simplifying devices, it is very difficult to make sense out of the random events that constitute reality. Controlling the narrative is a key objective of political life because public opinion is formed at this basic level. What happened to the global financial system in the 1930s was highly complex and shaped by many random events, but the dominant narrative that emerged was extremely easy to grasp. Selfish "economic royalists," to use Franklin Roosevelt's phrase, had been allowed to have their way at the expense of the little guy.

The latest financial crisis has spawned two competing narratives, each of which leads to drastically different policy prescriptions.

The dominant narrative of what caused the recent financial crisis (and this part is more implied than spoken) is that once upon a time the financial economy was regulated so that bad things did not happen to the little guy. Then George W. Bush deregulated the financial markets. This allowed evil (not merely stupid) bankers to make risky bets and sell risky products, including mortgages designed to go bad, out of unfettered greed. They brought the economy to its knees and were bailed out by the taxpayers, but tough regulations—such as the Dodd-Frank Wall Street Reform and Consumer Protection Act—have been put in place to protect the little guy and make sure something like this never happens again.

A competing narrative is far less frequently told outside the pages of the *Wall Street Journal*, although Gretchen Morgenson of *The New York Times* has, with mortgage expert Joshua Rosner, told it well in the book *Reckless Endangerment* (Times Books, 2011). It does not let greedy bankers off the hook, but maintains that to a large degree, the crisis was created through a mixture of bad if well-intended public policy and crony capitalism in the housing finance market. This narrative focuses on the GSEs we met in the last chapter, with a central role being played by Fannie Mae CEO Jim Johnson and a host of enablers in Congress and the Washington power structure, including Messrs. Dodd and Frank. In this tale, Fannie Mae and Freddie Mac became money-making machines for their managers by using their ambiguous status as "government-sponsored" public companies to borrow cheap (essentially at US government debt rates) at very high leverage to build enormous portfolios of mortgage securities. They used some of their vast income to buy bipartisan influence in Congress that shielded them from effective regulatory oversight. As a price of ongoing political support of their uncontestable ability to dominate the traditional "conforming" mortgage business through high leverage and low-cost funding, they acquiesced in increasingly loose standards of mortgage underwriting. As a direct result, Fannie and Freddie ended up guaranteeing trillions of dollars in mortgages, many of which should never have been written, and would not have been written without bipartisan political mandates to expand "affordable housing" to people with no job, no income, and no savings.

As I said above, this narrative doesn't let the Wall Street leverage machine off the hook, but bundling consumer debt—especially mortgages—into highly rated bonds had been going on without incident for a generation. Creating rotten mortgages for this financial sausage machine, more than the machine itself, underlay the crisis. Today Fannie and Freddie are more dominant in the US mortgage markets than ever and still have affordable housing mandates. Many Fannie and Freddie friends and protectors in Washington retain powerful positions.

Neither narrative is entirely adequate, though the second has the handicap of being complicated, too much so for the public to comprehend. Often what seems like villainy after a financial bubble has burst made great sense to all the participants at the time. Looking for villains to blame for misfortune is a function of common human nature, but after episodes of universal folly, everyone is guilty to some extent and nobody is a victim. The problem is that it is hard to have a compelling narrative without bad guys.

At the risk of spoiling a good story, nobody caused the financial crisis because everybody did. What went terribly wrong with finance is that it became too complacent, too complicated, and too concentrated at the same time over the course of the Great Moderation. New, quantitative approaches to managing and pricing risk, elegant computer simulations, and highly liquid global markets to distribute risk promised to move finance out of the dark ages of boom and bust. Governments of both the center-left and center-right embraced the finance-driven economy because it delivered the goods in the form of economic growth and job creation. The so-called Anglo-Saxon economies with their dynamic capital markets and global investment banks outpaced other developed economies in Europe and Asia. Bill Clinton and Tony Blair both enjoyed long periods in office and in return delivered "light-touch" regulation to the bankers who were among their largest financial supporters.

In *Financial Market Meltdown* (Praeger, 2009) I basically update the great Victorian banker and journalist Walter Bagehot, who wrote the great financial classic *Lombard Street* (1873), which tells the lay reader how finance works. I will not repeat myself here, but two points Bagehot insisted on remain true: First, banks need to be cautious and dull because they deal in other people's money, and an optimistic and complacent banker is more dangerous than an outright fraudster. Second, banking needs to be kept simple, and if it gets complicated, it goes wrong.

The banking practices of the Great Moderation violated both rules. The complacency is easy to understand given the willingness of governments to prevent banks from suffering more losses despite frequent financial crises. The complication, on the other hand, is knottier, and stems from two things: misguided attempts at establishing global capital adequacy in the banking system (the so-called Basel process), and attempts by the banks to become growth companies—something their shareholders demanded. There is nothing outlandish about either idea. In fact, nobody of consequence opposed them at the time. Concentration of the banking industry was not an object of these two mandates, but instead the inevitable result of them.

The Postwar Financial Order Undone

The Basel process, which is still underway, started with the near-death experience of the global financial system in the 1980s. To make a long story short, the relative financial stability that underpinned the postwar recovery of the world economy was based on a set of arrangements worked out at the conference of allied finance ministers (which effectively meant the United States and the United Kingdom) at Bretton Woods, New Hampshire, in 1944, with Lord Keynes providing many of the key concepts. To grossly simplify, in the Bretton Woods system, the world's currencies were effectively pegged to the US dollar in place of the old gold standard, but the US dollar had to maintain a link to gold. Bretton Woods created a new international institution, the International Monetary Fund (IMF), which pooled resources of participating countries in order to make funds available to help them make adjustments necessitated by balance-of-payment problems.

The key weakness in the Bretton Woods system was that it required monetary discipline on the part of the United States, whose dollar was in effect the new gold, the anchor for all other currencies. The United Kingdom understood its role as issuer of the global reserve currency and played it well until it could no longer afford it. The US government was and is inevitably driven by domestic politics to put its reserve currency obligations in second place at best. The simple fact was (and remains) that the US government could print money without limit if it chose to, and in the 1970s it did so with a vengeance to finance a vast expansion of social spending and the Vietnam War without raising taxes. Other countries got stiffed as America paid its bills in dollars of diminishing value. The Bretton Woods deal included a gold window, where dollar claims could be converted, but the United States lacked the gold. So, over a weekend, with no consultations, the United States blew up the Bretton Woods system, closing the gold window.

This kicked off the Great Inflation, and it ushered in an era of floating exchange rates that we are still living with today. OPEC, an attempt by oil producers to use cartel tactics to raise the price of their commodity (priced in dollars) in nominal terms to make up for the fall in the real value of the dollar, was a key side effect. The OPEC price hikes stuck, despite the fact that many countries could not afford them. To a large extent, this was made possible because the oil producers could do little with their dollars except deposit them in the American banks.

These banks, with US government encouragement, started "recycling" these so-called petro-dollars by lending them to countries to pay for oil imports, which then flowed back to the banks to make more loans. In other words, OPEC was essentially lending countries the money they needed to buy oil at the new prices. Had countries been unable to borrow petro-dollars, OPEC might not have been able to hold together for long. As it was, from 1973 through 1982, the sovereign lending market, centered in London, became the biggest single money-spinner for the largest US banks, and many international banks joined the party.

Walt Wriston, then CEO of First National City Bank of New York, acted as a sort of leader of the pack, telling everyone "countries do not go broke." Well, not quite, but they can stop paying banks what they owe, and there is precious little the banks can do about it. All these sovereign credits had interest rates floating above LIBOR, the interbank dollar loan rate in London. In 1982, the Fed jacked up interest rates to kill domestic inflation. LIBOR went through the roof, making scores of countries unable to pay what they owed. Many of the largest international banks had more bad loans to countries like Mexico, Argentina, and Brazil on their books than they had capital. Most were saved as the world's central banks and treasuries figured out how to restructure the loans, though Latin America suffered a "lost decade" of austerity and economic stagnation as sovereign markets' credit disappeared.

The Basel Process Is Born

Most regulation is a reaction to the last big disaster. The sovereign debt crisis of the 1980s convinced the developed world's central banks that consistent bank capital rules between countries were necessary to prevent another global crisis. This was only sensible, because many of the excesses of the sovereign debt crisis were the result of banks from countries such as Japan that had lenient capital regimes using that advantage to undercut their rival on price and otherwise erode market discipline. So the Basel process was born.

Basel, Switzerland, is home to an odd institutional relic of the interwar years: the Bank for International Settlements. Its original mission was to coordinate the activities of the central banks around the Dawes Plan, by which Germany essentially borrowed US money to pay reduced reparations to countries that had borrowed from the United States during the war. Like many international organizations, it just kept running after its reason for being had ceased to exist. As a preexisting club of central banks of the most important financial powers, it was an ideal forum for a common set of capital rules to be hammered out, though actual implementation was naturally a matter for national governments.

The product of the Basel Committee was an international agreement called Basel I, which set a standard of how much capital of what type (defined as "tiers") banks had to hold against what types of assets. For example, commercial loans, government bonds, and mortgages all had different capital weightings, so to achieve an acceptable overall capital ratio, banks could either adjust their mix of business or their mix and level of capital. This in theory would mean that capital levels—the first line of defense against bank failure—would be generally in line with the actual risks banks were undertaking. Most major banking countries adopted some or all of Basel I. The United States exempted all but large banks.

The problem was as always in the details. The world's banking systems are very different from each other. Basel of necessity had to accommodate this fact while writing one-size-fits-all rules that national governments, influenced by their domestic banking lobbies, were willing to accept. Therefore, government debt was given a zero capital weight, largely because many countries relied on banks, not their local bond markets, to buy their debt. Bank lending to other banks also got lenient treatment. Bank lending to the business sector was given higher weights, as was lending to households.

In a world without financial innovation—and, it might be added, financial markets insisting on very high returns on capital—such a regime might have produced a more stable financial system. But the United States had already developed a finance-driven economy in which both governments at all levels and the top tier of corporations had direct access to the capital markets. This process, called by the ugly term "disintermediation," had become entrenched well before the Basel process. In fact, it was a factor in the embrace of sovereign debt lending by the largest US banks whose core corporate banking franchise had been eroding throughout the 1970s due to competition from the bonds and commercial paper issued by Wall Street firms—a competition that banking systems in other countries did not face to any degree.

The Birth of Consumer Banking

Walt Wriston, who had spotted the sovereign-debt El Dorado, became at about the same time in the early 1970s one of the first bankers to notice a key development in the US "flow-of-funds" data. Unlike the situation prevailing in the 1950s and early 1960s, when big institutions, governments, and corporations held a lion's share of financial assets and income, by the 1970s the household sector was capturing an increasing share of the national balance sheet and income. The new El Dorado was to be consumer or retail banking, a business that large US commercial banks had by and large ignored.

US banks faced huge obstacles in this business. Unlike other countries, the United States had laws and regulations that made expansion across state lines impossible, and only a few states allowed even statewide branching. The US government had fostered a whole industry—the savings-and-loan (S&L), or "thrift," industry—to provide housing finance under favorable regulatory treatment. These factors ruled out the obvious routes to acquiring customers and making loans by building physical branch networks. The answer was a uniquely American innovation, the bank credit card.

What is innovative about the credit card is not the idea of an embossed card linking an individual to a revolving credit account. Retailers had been issuing charge cards to their good customers for generations. What was innovative was the radical severing of the credit account from a specific merchant/ customer relationship on one hand and the equally radical severing of bank credit underwriting from a branch-based customer relationship on the other. Suddenly banks could efficiently make personal loans to individuals the bank had no other relationships with beyond issuing them the card. This was only made possible by building a new business system: the so-called bankcard association or card scheme. This was a voluntary, self-regulating body that ran a franchise governed by rules for banks issuing cards, banks accepting and discounting card transactions from merchants, and the merchants themselves. As technology advanced, the card schemes also developed data networks to automate the flow of information between the parties, but the guts of the system consisted of the so-called four-party model, which allowed a merchant—any retailer or service provider—to make a credit sale to an individual about whom they knew nothing except that they were a person with a valid card. The merchant's bank is paid by the bank issuing the credit card through card association channels and pays a net amount to the merchant. The card association essentially acts as a vast global clearinghouse operated outside of conventional national payment systems.

The reason for the card association model, and why the US banks stumbled into it, was precisely the extreme geographical fragmentation of the US banking system (there were 25,000 or so banks in the 1970s, only a handful of them able to draw on the significant local market). One of these exceptions was California, where BankAmericard was launched in the 1960s as the first bank credit card. Other banks saw its success, but did not want to participate in a business controlled by a rival. So they established an association to pool resources. BankAmericard had to follow suit, resulting in the two rival global card brands we know today, MasterCard and Visa. At first, the credit card business was both widespread among US banks and fairly marginal. Banks still were in the main issuing cards to their own customers, and largely as an efficient way of making small consumer loans.

From the mid-1960s to the mid-1980s, growth was slow, largely because of the classic chicken-and-the-egg problem: cards were of limited utility until most merchants accepted them for payment, but merchants had little incentive to accept them until a critical mass of their customers had cards and wanted to use them. One persistent problem was that most states had usury laws that made the small-loans business, which required a high interest spread to offset the high defaults that characterize retail credit, unattractive when market interest rates were high. During the great inflation of the 1970s and early 1980s, market rates for bank funding often were close to or above usury ceilings.

For example, in New York, the usury ceiling for consumer loans was 12 percent, and the bank cost of funds was at one point touching 20 percent. The credit card lenders were bleeding to death. Saving the day was Walt Wriston, or the Governor of South Dakota, depending on who is telling the story. A unanimous 1978 decision of the US Supreme Court in the case *Marquette National Bank of Minneapolis vs. First of Omaha Service Corporation* had ruled that if a bank was chartered in a state, that state's laws governed its right to charge interest no matter where a borrower might reside. Several states had either no usury laws or very high ceilings, and South Dakota set out deliberately to become the credit card capital of the world by writing the most favorable legislation. First National City Bank of New York created a South Dakota bank to issue cards in 1981. Other states including Delaware got into the game, and soon a pattern became established where most cards were issued to borrowers nationwide out of a handful of friendly states.

Once free of state usury laws, banks could charge interest according to the actuarial risk of default a customer represented, something we consumers know as our credit score. This meant that it became feasible to offer credit to millions of strangers nationwide through targeting mailings based on statistical analysis. Only the largest card businesses had the resources to build the required skills and infrastructure, and the larger the card portfolio, the more the law of large numbers spread costs and risks. As a result, the credit card industry became consolidated into a relatively few banks within a decade. As wholesale banking continued to lose ground to the capital markets, and as the largest banks were still trying to write off their sovereign debt overhang, the credit card business became the single most lucrative activity in US banking, which before the 1980s had left consumer credit to the retailers, consumer finance companies, and loan sharks. To a large extent, Wriston and his successor John Reed gave their bank the raw earning power to dig its way out from its sovereign debt problems through its bold and early drive into the card business.

Safe As Houses

A second front in expanding the retail side of US banking opened up in the 1980s. The New Deal had created an S&L industry and a slew of government mortgage programs that more or less monopolized the mortgage business. The key was something called Regulation Q, which set deposit interest rates for commercial banks and S&Ls. S&Ls were allowed to pay 1/4 percent more than banks, so they had an inside track on collecting household savings to fund mortgages. When Federal Reserve Chairman Paul Volcker pumped up rates to break the fever of the Great Inflation, the bank prime rate hit 21.5 percent. Banks were only allowed to pay depositors 5 percent and S&Ls 5 1/4 percent. Depositors fled both, as the brokerage industry invented money market funds, which offered market rates.

Congress phased out Regulation Q in the early 1980s (though the prohibition on paying interest on demand accounts remained until recently) and materially raised deposit insurance. This set off a dangerous competition for deposits based on high rates, a competition that attracted a lot of opportunistic and fickle hot money into the banks offering them. Congress also allowed the S&L industry to enter more lines of business, including commercial real estate lending. As a group, the S&Ls were challenged to find loans that would generate returns sufficient to cover their funding costs, and many turned to speculative property developers as customers. Regulators were concerned, but the industry had ironclad political support on both sides of the aisle. This bought them time and "regulatory forbearance," but by 1989 the whole S&L industry had to be bailed out by Congress through establishing a special asset management company called the Resolution Trust Corporation (RTC) to acquire and dispose of the assets, mostly real estate loans, of failed banks. Hundreds of institutions disappeared, leaving the S&L industry a shadow of its former self. This created a gap in mortgage provision, thus presenting a second major consumer credit opportunity for commercial banks. By the 1990s, most large commercial banks had established mortgage-banking subsidiaries to fill the void left by traditional mortgage lenders.

By the later 1990s, most of the revenue in US commercial banking was being earned by lending money to households. To put this in perspective, for the whole time since commercial joint-stock banks were first established in the late 18th and early 19th centuries, their business was providing working capital to industry and commerce. They bundled the savings of many households to make commercial and industrial loans. By 1990, their principal business was consumer lending, an activity once called money-lending—something that old-line commercial bankers would be put off by, and that banks in Europe and Japan did very little of, since commercial banking was still viable.

Risky Business

There was a third pool of revenue that expanded rapidly for the largest US banks in the 1990s: a bundle of activities collectively known as treasury and trading. Since banks are both repositories and wholesalers of the deposit money of the rest of the economy, a treasury function of some sort is always needed. It used to be fairly simple: selling excess funds to other banks or buying funds from them to fill the gaps between loans and deposits. Banks used to try the best they could to match the length of their loans to the "duration" of their deposits and other funding sources, such as bonds. This is one of the reasons commercial banks stayed away from long-term loans and mortgages until recent decades. Once interest rates were deregulated, how banks funded themselves in the market and, especially, what degree of mismatch between loans and funding they were willing to risk, became an important way of making higher profits. Treasury became a "profit center," not a utility function, in the largest banks.

Trading income was also scarce before the collapse of Bretton Woods created a world of floating exchange rates. The value of any currency vs. any other currency became a second-to-second market determination. Interbank trading of foreign exchange became one of the largest markets in the world, and remains such, with trillions turning over every day. Again, a new profit center for the largest banks was born. Although the real commercial needs of customers were at the bottom of all this activity, most bank trading desks were mainly engaged in proprietary trading, betting the bank's own capital. As time went on, this expanded into other markets, such as financial futures, bonds, and even commodities.

On the whole, the general public, politicians, and regulators tend to think that a bank is a bank, and though few understand how a bank really works, they assume that it makes its living taking deposits and making loans. And for most banks except the largest, this remains true. But by 1990, the largest banks had become dependent on businesses that had scarcely existed before 1980: highly specialized business "silos" that had little to do with each other—or for that matter, little to do with banking as it had been practiced for centuries. Treasury and trading activities, mortgages, and credit cards were essentially independent of the local branches or operating subsidiaries required by the traditional "geographical" bank businesses of deposit taking and lending. The old US laws, both state and federal, which had long limited the size of banks by limiting their geographical scope, didn't matter anymore.

The only constraint these businesses faced was that every bank had only so much capital; indeed, the task of bank management increasingly became a matter of allocating capital to the businesses that had the greatest returns. And this is where the Basel process came into play. Some activities, such as consumer lending, had very high returns but also high capital requirements, whereas bank-to-bank trading did not. Since return on invested capital is key in a finance-driven economy, the use of the bank's own balance sheet became problematic. The answer to this dilemma was yet another financial innovation, asset securitization. This was a fancy way of describing a process by which a bundle of loans is taken off the books of a bank, packaged as a debt security, and sold into the market. It was invented in the 1970s for mortgages, but the mechanism got extended to auto loans, credit card loans, and the like, as moving assets off the bank balance sheet became a key tactic in generating more revenue with less capital. Ironically, the retail loans that got tough capital requirement under Basel were, thanks to the law of large numbers and the modest sums at risk for each, capable of being managed on an actuarial basis. In other words, losses were statistically predictable. Other assets, like interbank and government loans, were much larger exposures and harder to predict.

The Triumph of the Market

By the 1990s, the largest banks—at least in the United States—had become cogs in a "market-centric" financial system in which the capital markets provided the bulk of their funding and purchased a very large proportion of the assets they generated. The bank role was to "originate" assets such as credit card loans and mortgages through "channels" such as direct mail, home banking, and specialized sales forces (e.g., mortgage brokers). These assets would be "packaged" into securities investment banks and sold, held in portfolio, and traded. Increasingly, banks came to play more of these capital market roles themselves as the constraints of the Depression-era Glass-Steagall Act (which strictly separated commercial and investment banking) were allowed to lapse by degrees. The old core functions of the bank were relatively unremunerative compared to this "originate, manufacture, and distribute" model.

Regulators were becoming increasingly comfortable with the "market-centric" model too, because the securities churned out had to be properly vetted and rated by the credit agencies under SEC (Securities and Exchange Commission) rules. Moreover, distributing risk to large numbers of sophisticated institutions seemed safer than leaving it concentrated on the books of individual banks. Besides, even the Basel-process experts had become convinced that bank risk management had reached a new level of effectiveness through the use of sophisticated statistical models, and the Basel II rules that superseded Basel I especially allowed the largest and most sophisticated banks to use approved models to set their capital requirements.

The fly in the ointment of market-centric finance was that it allowed an almost infinite expansion of credit in the economy, but creditworthy risks are by definition finite. At some point, every household with a steady income has seven credit cards, a mortgage, and a home equity line. What then? Unlike the utility-banking model of the past, where banks were expected to earn modest but steady returns on their capital, the financial markets now demanded that banks produce high returns on capital and grow briskly. Returns on capital could be boosted by increasing the leverage in the balance sheet by borrowing more and buying back shares, but Basel regulatory capital set a limit to all that. However, compared to historical levels, banks became leveraged to the hilt through creative capital structures. Growth was a bigger challenge as long as barriers to interstate bankers and mergers were in place. In the wake of the S&L crisis, however, a broad swath of states and localities found local banking systems poisoned by bad loans or shut down by the Federal Deposit Insurance Corporation (FDIC). The political power of local banking franchises that was once used in Washington and state capitals to keep big competitors out swung into reverse. Many local banks wanted (or had) to be bought to stay open. The barriers fell in stages, beginning with interstate compacts.

The result was a consolidation of American banking that resembled a game of Pac-Man. Banks that developed efficient acquisition engines, some from unlikely places like Rhode Island, Ohio, and North Carolina, became adept at using a high stock price to buy a target bank, take a restructuring reserve, strip out costs ruthlessly while holding on to most assets and customers, release the reserve to boost earnings and stock prices, and then devour the next bank. This is nothing new—Walter Bagehot noted that unless constrained, a large bank will always get larger—but in the United Kingdom, it took 120 years for the scores of joint-stock banks to consolidate into a half-dozen big ones. Pac-Man banking, on the other hand, consolidated most of the US industry into less than a dozen megabanks and "super-regional" players in the course of a decade.

Despite the protests of Occupy Wall Street, in this whole story there is less greed (granting that bank CEOs are paid by the size of their empires and did as a group become very wealthy) than market logic, where institutional investors demanded that banks either produce high-yield growth stocks or be taken over and dismembered by those that did. These institutional investors are, of course, managing our own insurance and retirement savings. Banks did not become bad in a moral sense—dealing in money is no more or less moral than any other commercial activity—but they became for all intents and purposes unmanageable for two reasons.

First, they ceased being the radically simple business that Walter Bagehot described in *Lombard Street*, where all a banker had to do was exercise extreme caution in lending out his depositor's money. In fact, every business, from credit card to trading in the capital markets, became incredibly specialized and opaque to general management and boards of directors, much less security analysts. Only a handful of senior bankers—Jamie Dimon of J. P. Morgan Chase comes to mind, despite recent lapses in risk management at the bank—could be said to have a firm grip on the details of their constituent businesses and the risks in their balance sheets.

Second, they became too large to manage effectively—something called "diseconomies of scale"—so bureaucracies and overheads multiplied, with bouts of reorganizations and head-count reductions as a periodic corrective. Innovation, customer service, and the ability to react to new competitors (except to buy them and kill them) all suffered from gigantism.

Given where the industry had arrived by 2007, the remarkable thing is not that there was a banking crisis on the scale we experienced, but that one didn't occur earlier.

How Government Policy and Central Banks Shaped the Market Meltdown

As mentioned at the beginning of this chapter, the dominant narrative has it that the greedy banks on Wall Street somehow caused the crisis in the financial markets by taking reckless risks in pursuit of outsized bonuses. There is much truth in that allegation. But the reality is actually worse: the top management of the largest banks by and large didn't understand the risks on their balance sheets and trading desks. But, then, given the complicated beasts banks had become, who could? Certainly the regulators of banks and financial markets, both here and in other major financial centers, did not have a clue of what really went on inside the financial sausage factory. Even, if they were clever enough to understand it, the vastly greater rewards of being in the financial economy most likely had already brought them over to the side of those they regulated. There is no evidence that this has changed nor any reason to believe it will ever change. NBA stars make more than referees, right?

The dominant narrative also blames something called deregulation for the meltdown and even insists that it occurred under George W. Bush. There is not a scintilla of truth to this, though through repetition it is widely accepted. Again, I'll stipulate that it is true that things went badly in the realm of public policy and regulation, but these were not the things the narrative insists upon—indeed, quite the opposite.

Deregulation of finance began when the Great Inflation of the Nixon-Carter era made interest-rate setting by the government—also known as financial repression—untenable. With inflation running at 15 percent or more, capping savings rates at 5 percent was effectively liquidating the value of the savings held in banks by the public. The problem was that the public was voting with its feet and pouring resources into mutual funds and other investments, threatening the ability of the banking system to fund itself and make loans. When deregulation essentially completed with Bill Clinton's signature of the Graham-Leach-Bliley Act of 1999, the financial crisis of 2008 was nearly a decade in the future. If deregulation caused the crisis, the timing is strange, to say the least. There is no cause and effect because there never is a case where regulation or its absence causes anything.

Regulation is a process of deciding what activities government will permit or forbid players in a market to perform and how. Capping interest rates was intended to make banking safe, but the unintended consequence was that banks became unable to function when inflation got out of hand. The rule didn't cause the Great Inflation; bad government policy did. The Great Inflation probably accelerated the transfer of financial activity from banks to the capital markets, and so-called deregulation was in large measure an after-the-fact effort of the regulators, notably the Fed, to keep the banks they supervised in the game which had shifted to the great advantage of capital markets players.

More recently, the rise in home prices that led to the 2008 crisis had less to do with the banks and how they were regulated than it did with the 70 years of government policy promoting home ownership and a series of financial innovations that made home loans more affordable. Banks participated in the home finance machine because it was large, profitable, and seemed a one-way bet. Prices of houses in most markets had never gone down in living memory. In other words, the banks believed the same things that homebuyers and politicians believed. Financial panics and crises are almost never caused by what everyone thinks is dangerous, but by what everyone believes to be safe. And we never ban or restrict what is thought to be safe.

Regulation can in itself be more dangerous than its absence. Machiavelli instructs his prince that nothing is more perilous than managing a change in the order of things. Between the 1960s and the 1980s, a change in the order of things quietly took hold in finance. Put simply, the "Anglo-Saxon" world moved from a financial system where regulated banks were the key providers of credit and held the savings of the public to a system where the capital markets took center stage. The rest of the world remained more bank centered at home, but all large financial institutions increasingly found themselves operating in a global market for capital that by and large played by "Anglo-Saxon" rules. This capital market had clusters or nodes of real people and offices in a few hub cities such as New York and London, but it was essentially a product of modern information technology and operated 24 hours a day on blinking computer screens. How to effectively identify and control risks in this global electronic market was a new problem for regulators, and it belonged to everybody and nobody.

Meanwhile, traditional financial regulations assumed a world of national systems centered on banks. Even the Basel process, for all its international cooperation, essentially focused on how banks should be regulated, especially with respect to capital standards, by national authorities.

The reality of the financial economy was and remains an entirely different world than that imagined by the regulators and their political masters. In the global financial market, a retiree with her money in an "ultra-safe" money market mutual fund is often unknowingly lending her dollars to European banks so they can buy and sell dollar assets, including Triple A mortgage-backed bonds or their derivatives. The mortgages backing the bonds might be NINJA (no income, no job, no assets) loans made by a broker claiming, as many did, that they could "get a mortgage approved for a ham sandwich."

The Triple A–rated bonds would collapse in value as house prices in America stopped going up because supply outstripped people who could afford a house, even on ridiculously easy "liar-loan" standards. Once prices stopped going up, market participants began to realize that these Triple A securities were going to head south in a hurry. Liar loans didn't much matter when the house was worth more than the loan and kept going up in value. At best, the overextended borrowers could refinance the mortgage; at worst they would default, but the foreclosed house was marketable at a price that repaid the lender. Falling house prices made an increasing number of homes worth less than the loans involved, and rising defaults and foreclosures drove down prices further.

This is how bubbles deflate. Had the US banks held the mortgages on their own books, as they do in most markets, only the domestic market would have tanked, as it did in the S&L crisis of the 1980s. However, the financial sausage factory had turned the bulk of them into securities held by investors all over the world, including banks, insurance companies, and the giant US government-sponsored enterprises whose straight debt was also held by banks and central banks worldwide. Individual market players had not only to worry about what time bombs might be in their own portfolios—and they often had many uncoordinated trading and investment businesses around the world—but what other banks they dealt with in overnight money market lending might have in theirs. In a boom everyone trusts everyone; in a bust nobody trusts anybody. The rates at which banks made overnight loans to each other began rising to unheard of rates in August of 2007, over a year before Lehman went bust. It was the canary in the mine.

The Classic Cure for Financial Panics

Now, there is no great mystery what to do to stop a panic in one marketplace. Every country has a central bank that can backstop its domestic banking system by loaning the banks enough money to meet their obligations. When the players know that they are going to be paid what is owed to them, they will pay what they owe others, and stark fear will subside while the authorities "resolve" the hopeless cases, winding down the businesses or selling off the bits. When banks in the euro zone are stuffed with toxic dollar paper sold to them by investment banks, and other banks won't give them overnight loans and the money market funds won't buy their IOUs either, things get more than a little complicated. The markets are too seamlessly interconnected—too big for the old playbook to work.

When it was first spelled out by Walter Bagehot in *Lombard Street*, the idea that one bank (in his case, the Bank of England) could hold the reserves of the whole banking system and lend without stint in a panic against all valid claims (commonly called the "lender of last resort" role) was controversial but highly practical. Bank credit was a small percentage of GDP, as little at 5 percent. In 2007, UK bank assets were 500 percent of GDP. Many, indeed most, of these assets were in dollars and other currencies. The Bank of England can only create money in sterling, so it can't act as lender of last resort, even to the UK banking system. In fact, only one possible lender of last resort exists in the global financial economy: the US Federal Reserve System. The problem of course is that it didn't (and doesn't) have the authority to do what needs to be done under any circumstances, which is exactly what a lender of last resort must do. What it does have is the global reserve currency, meaning the currency most other countries keep their surplus in and often peg their currencies against. That means that it can blow up the size of its balance sheet by buying assets from the banking system to an almost infinite degree—what is often called "printing money." Few other central banks could do this without debasing the currency they issued, including the shiny new European Central Bank, which needed to establish its credibility.

The problem with the Fed as lender of last resort is that the American people and their representatives in Congress will never put up with it doing the right thing. This was a fast-moving crisis, nobody had the information they needed, and only the Fed had sufficient muscle to act. But it didn't have the tools. Part of the gap between the reality of the global financial economy and regulation was that regulation was still living in a world where different agencies had responsibility for institutions, products, and markets that had in reality been hopelessly blurred by technology and market forces. The SEC, the FDIC, the Commodity Futures Exchange Commission (CTFC), the Controller of the

Currency, and the Federal Reserve all held pieces of turf and all had friends in Congress (and at the firms they regulated), so nobody had complete information or discretion to act, with the possible exception of the US Treasury and the president. However, they needed specific authority from Congress to take bold and open-ended action to stem the crisis.

At first, Henry Paulson was naive enough to ask Congress for what was really needed: a carte blanche to use a big chunk of federal cash to do anything that needed to be done to stop the panic. Congress, as former member Jim Leach—one of the few who really understood the world of finance—once put it, always acts with "bovine incomprehension" when confronted with an issue involving banks and money. This is unfair to cows. Congress in fact always channels a popular American suspicion and loathing of banks and bankers that goes back to Jefferson and Jackson. Both left and right refused Paulson's blank check in a decisive legislative rebuff that made their constituents feel good and accelerated the panic worldwide.

The resulting chaos convinced Congress to authorize the Troubled Asset Relief Program (TARP), a far more complex and unwieldy mechanism. The plot behind it was that the Treasury would buy up mortgage securities and thereby set a floor on their value and restart the markets, preventing banks from going broke from their bad bets in the process. This quickly proved impossible to implement, since the instruments in question were too complex and opaque to be valued. Plan B was to inject the TARP funds directly into the banks as capital. Direct capital infusions had been tried and had to an extent worked in Europe; notably, the United Kingdom. As a general rule, history suggests that pumping capital directly into a bank that the market fears is insolvent—that is, can never pay its bills—can buy time if nothing else. To avoid playing favorites and singling out the weakest banks, the Treasury and Fed essentially forced all the banks to accept injections of TARP funds in proportion to their size. The public and much of Congress hates TARP, but it broke the fever of the panic, which came very close to taking the entire global financial economy over the edge.

The government response suffered from one huge handicap beyond the public's visceral outrage at "bailing out" the banks: namely, misdiagnosing the disease. Very few people in the general public or Congress understand that since the 1930s, no money has existed in society beyond deposits on the books of banks. Without deposit taking banks, there is no money, and no economy.

Nobody could understand that the financial economy faced a solvency crisis rather than a liquidity crisis, the difference between being dead broke and being in need of a loan to buy time and restore confidence. The classic tonic for a liquidity crisis is to lower interest rates and flood the market with money until assets that looked risky look cheap and banks begin trading again—and easy money improves business confidence. Almost every financial crisis and recession between 1945 and 2008 had responded to this medicine.

The tonic—essentially pumping money into the system until trading and lending resumes—simply doesn't work if the banks are unable to pay what they owe to depositors and counterparties. Then the only answer is to move quickly to put them out of their misery quickly and with as little harm to others as possible. The FDIC is very good at doing this with small banks, and even middling ones.

However, in the 1990s the US banking industry became very concentrated in the top ten or so banks for reasons noted above. The investment banks went from partnerships to public companies and also got very, very large. The global financial markets became so intertwined that these institutions were exposed to every other bank of every size and vice versa. This situation is often called "too big to fail" because all these complex interconnections between market players are impossible to understand in detail but clearly have the potential to bring down everybody if a really big institution suddenly ceased paying what they owed the other banks. The problem during the crisis was that it was not at all obvious who could be allowed to go to the wall and who had to be saved at all costs. There was no clear set of principles or policies to be applied. As the solvency of one large institution after another came into question, the markets pushed them quickly toward failure by cutting off liquidity and credit. Each case, starting with Bear Stearns, was essentially handled ad hoc, and this very seat-of-the-pants crisis management unnerved already panic-stricken markets. Oddly, it also emboldened the managers of some highly regarded firms to hang tough, especially Lehman. If the authorities rescued Bear Stearns, a distinctly down-market franchise deep in the mortgage mire, surely they would not let Lehman fail.

Of course, the US government did let Lehman fail, partially because the Federal Reserve did not have the authority it needed to bail out an investment bank. But the authorities also feared that doing so—and in effect reinforcing the idea that no major firm would be allowed to fail under any circumstances—would give rise to an extremely dangerous level of moral hazard in the financial markets. *Moral hazard* is an economic term for how people behave when their actions have no downside. Successful and often repeated rescues of the financial economy during the Greenspan years had led to a situation of "Heads, I win; tails, the government pays." Sometimes this is referred to as private profits and socialized losses, and even deposit insurance is tainted with the same problem. If the government will make you whole when a bank fails, why not deposit your savings with the bank offering the highest rates, even if it might be a bit dodgy?

History suggests that the way to deal with a solvency crisis is to do a swift and brutal triage of the banks, taking over the whole system temporarily if necessary. J. P. Morgan did this personally in the Panic of 1907, and Sweden did it in 1992. The problem in 2008 was that the financial economy was too big, and was globally interconnected in ways that made it difficult for any one government to take this on alone, and international policy coordination was beyond the ability of national authorities to orchestrate amid a fast-moving market panic. In the end, the authorities in the leading financial countries muddled through by marrying dying banks to ones that still had a pulse and taking direct ownership of the hopeless, such as Fannie Mae and Freddie Mac. The UK government, at vast expense, ended up owning its two largest domestic bank groups.

It is easy with 20/20 hindsight to be critical of men and women scrambling to keep financial Armageddon at bay. What did emerge from all the skin-of-our-teeth crisis management, however, were three key facts.

First, the too-big-to-fail institutions ended up even bigger and became almost impossible to manage. The Japanese banking crisis had resulted in something similar.

Second, vast amounts of public money spent on the bank bailouts and driving interest rates to record lows left the authorities with little ammunition in case the crisis took a turn for the worse—indeed, countries such as Ireland were driven to the brink by guarantees of banking system deposits.

Third, the publics of all the countries affected were alienated and angered by the entire process, greatly limiting the options the national government would have available if the crisis entered a new phase.

Why Things Might Get Worse

Americans are a forgiving people, but also a vindictive one when they feel swindled. The problem with the housing bubble and subsequent meltdown was that everyone thought that rising house prices would go on forever. A few brave souls warned of a bubble but were largely ignored. Families and speculators alike lied about their qualification for mortgages, brokers helped them document the lies, banks invented no-money-down, adjustable-rate mortgages that looked affordable, and investment banks packed the loans into securities that magically turned lousy credit risks into Triple A bonds, thanks to the credit rating agencies who blessed the structures. Moreover, mortgage insurers—both private firms and the GSEs—"enhanced" the Rube Goldberg–structured loans with policies limiting the downside for investors in these securities. Everyone got what they wanted: homeowners lived in houses they couldn't afford; politicians took credit for record levels of home ownership; the home construction industry was provided millions of jobs; and brokers, banks, lawyers, appraisers, and home inspectors raked in hundreds of millions in fees.

When the music stopped, the shock to the economy and tens of millions of citizens' well-being and expectations was devastating. As in the wake of the Great Crash of 1929, villains had to be found and punished. The collective delusion of the housing bubble and market forces would not suffice as an explanation for such a calamity. However, there was no single person or group of identifiable individuals to put in the dock, as Ken Lay and Jeff Skilling had been after the collapse of Enron. The discovery and prosecution of Bernie Madoff was a poor substitute, since his Ponzi scheme far predated the bubble and had nothing to do with it. No, finance and, more broadly, greed, were to blame. The general public were of course victims, and the political class would avenge them and see that never again would something like the meltdown be allowed to occur. The first order of business, though, was to get back to the world of growth and debt-driven prosperity that after a quarter century everyone took as normal, even as a birthright. This meant the revival of the playbook devised by John Maynard Keynes during the Great Depression. Massive government stimulus would put cash in the hands of consumers and restore economic activity in the short run, even at the expense of taking on vastly higher levels of public debt. The fact that this had been tried and failed in the wake of the Japanese banking collapse of the 1990s didn't matter, because it could be argued Japan did too little too late. And to be fair, massive stimulus spending in China actually did prevent a steep downturn there. When private demand collapses suddenly, not replacing it with public-sector demand risks an uncontrolled downward spiral like that of the early Depression years, something that Ben Bernanke and other students of that era were determined to prevent.

The practical problem with substituting public-sector demand for private demand as Keynes advocated is that to work effectively, two things have to be in place that were missing in 2008–2009. First, it is helpful to have excess private savings that can be lured back into spending once the government takes the lead. Second, it is essential to have a banking system capable of transmitting the stimulus and amplifying its effects through lending. Both of these conditions more or less applied in the late 1930s in Britain, when Keynes proposed his remedy, which was a solution that was specific to a time and place, not a panacea. The British banks were intact and there was lots of private savings. In Depression-era America, the banking system had largely collapsed and vast amounts of paper wealth had evaporated by 1933, shattering confidence and making recovery much more challenging.

In the United States of 2008–2009, the balance sheets of large companies were by and large in good shape. The household balance sheet, however, was buried under a mountain of consumer debt and had lost $14 trillion in wealth—a whole year's worth of GDP and many times the public-sector budget. Until the household balance sheet became sustainable—meaning some balance between debt and income was achieved—restoring consumer spending was unlikely to respond to short-term infusions of government cash. This would probably be true even if the stimulus program had been properly sized, designed, and targeted, and few would argue it was. It may have been simultaneously too small and not focused directly on employing displaced workers where they were concentrated. We will never really know.

The larger problem was that the finance-driven economy's leverage machine had more or less ceased to function, both in the United States, which was ground zero of the crisis, and in Europe, where so much of the toxic assets had ended up on bank balance sheets. Putting capital into the banks and performing shotgun weddings had arrested the freefall, but the asset securitization market for consumer credit had virtually disappeared. Banks dared not take risks with their own capital, and the newly zealous bank regulators reinforced this caution. Good quality borrowers did not want to borrow.

Under the circumstances, it was not unreasonable to offset depressed private-sector demand by government spending until the "deleveraging" of the economy from under a mountain of private debt ran its course. Something had to be done. However, given the state of the banking "transmission" mechanism, all that a vast increase in public debt accomplished was to set the stage for the second and potentially worse leg of the crisis, a crisis in public finances.

The Lessons of the Great Depression Unlearned

Financial historian and journalist Amity Shlaes wrote a brilliant book on the New Deal, *The Forgotten Man*, which came out in June of 2007, just before the crisis was breaking over the financial economy. The New Deal has a place in American progressive iconography unlike any other in our history, as does Franklin Delano Roosevelt, its patron saint. The New Deal can best be understood as the third American founding. The 1789 founding resulted in a tension between the Hamiltonians, who wanted a strong European-style state led by natural aristocrats, and the Jeffersonians, who believed in limited federal government and a broad yeoman democracy based in the states. The second founding was the triumph of the Union in the Civil War, which strengthened the federal government relative to the states, but gave it little role in the economy, until the progressive era in the early 20th century introduced the Federal Reserve System and the income tax.

The New Deal firmly asserted the federal government's role in social and economic reconstruction and the guaranteed provision of a social safety net. Insofar as history is still taught in school, the New Deal is presented as an unalloyed good, with an activist government saving the country from the failures of business and Herbert Hoover. In place of evil businessmen, the New Deal empowered experts and established programs to manage the economy in the interests of the little guy. Economic democracy was the logical extension of political democracy.

Ms. Shlaes's book is a useful corrective to this narrative, looking at the impact of activist and intrusive government on the forgotten man: the entrepreneur and taxpayer who paid for it. She makes the case that a combination of powerful new federal bureaucracies, contradictory monetary policy experiments, expanding regulation, and massively higher taxes, combined with legislation that raised the cost of labor, inhibited economic recovery in the private economy. Despite unprecedented increases in public spending, the US economy was as bad in 1938 as it was in 1933, and real recovery only took place with the build up to World War II. Her contrarian view is that the markets would have cleared and healed faster if the country had been spared the frenetic energies of the New Dealers who undermined growth industries such as electrical utilities, and undermined the confidence of entrepreneurs and investors. We will never know, although we can note that the recovery from a steep post–World War I recession was accompanied by reductions in government regulation, spending, and taxes.

The Great Depression, it can be argued, was effectively institutionalized as an ongoing emergency that allowed programs and policies to be enacted that progressive politicians, intellectuals, and trade unionists had wanted to put in place for decades. Reordering the economy and the balance of economic power was deemed by some more important than improving business conditions and employment. In fact, expanding dependency of the population on the federal government was politically desirable, as was unionization of the workforce and high levels of taxation on "the rich" and corporations. The relentless attack on business and capital that FDR cranked up for his 1936 reelection was successful at the polls but also effective in terrifying investors and employers. If social reconstruction becomes the primary goal of politicians, their interest may not be served by allowing the markets to heal themselves. One does not have to accept Shlaes's reading of the New Deal era uncritically to be concerned about the precedents it established.

Three Years On: Why So Little Has Changed

Fortunately, there is a relatively benign explanation for the failure of government policy in the wake of the crash: all-too-human blundering all around. Blundering has not been by any means limited to the American political class. Europe and Japan have also suffered from inept and weak political leadership. Above all, the bankers themselves have failed to take responsibility for the widespread economic suffering caused by the crisis. The blunder here is that even if the dominant narrative is full of distortions and half-truths—and arguably it is—it can be easily understood by a financially illiterate public who are in very real distress. The course of wisdom, even decency, for bankers would have been to put on the hair shirt and eschew bonuses and perks for an interval sufficient for rage to subside. Nothing of the sort happened. Banks continued their lavish pay and bonuses as soon as they could repay their TARP injections, despite the fact that their return to positive results in 2010 was effectively engineered by the Federal Reserve, which offered them virtually free money with which they could buy bonds that provided a positive spread. Their phalanx of K Street lobbyists are seen fighting to eviscerate financial reforms without presenting a coherent alternative based on constructive reform of their own institutions and industry.

Deep down in the reptilian brains of the surviving high rollers of the financial bubble was a belief that the world of the Great Moderation was somehow normal and that things would return to normal as soon as the recovery from recession kicked into gear. A fundamental rethink of the business of finance from first principles was not called for or even conceivable. While this is scarcely surprising given common human nature, it was regrettable because the banks were setting themselves up as stock villains for the political class to attack, an event that is never constructive. I return to this point in Chapter 7.

Political Missteps

In politics as in war, overwhelming victory can lead the victors into hubris and disaster. The overwhelming landslide of 1932 had led to the golden age of the New Deal and almost continuous Democratic control of the House of Representatives for over 60 years. The march of state control over economy and society was slowed in the 1980s and '90s, but never really rolled back, despite a series of Republican presidential victories. In 2009, the Democrats gained control of the presidency and both houses of Congress, with decisive majorities. They had last enjoyed such a position in the Lyndon Johnson era. Like the victorious general who has routed the opposing army, they had vast numbers of potential objectives in reach.

Had it made the decision to focus on restoring business confidence and activity, this united government could have attempted to accomplish a great deal. There was the opportunity to simultaneously increase temporary income support while making pro-growth reforms in the tax code and providing a road map to sustainable public finances, something the bipartisan Simpson-Bowles Commission sketched out. Even an increase in direct government purchases of military hardware might have helped, as it did after 1940. So would a plan to let the financial, especially the mortgage, markets clear through actually finding a bottom at which assets would find ready buyers. The window for bold action with bipartisan support was there, as it was in 1933.

Whatever one thinks of the New Deal, Roosevelt treated the Depression as a national emergency equivalent to war and focused on nothing else in his famous 100 days. One of Roosevelt's best early strokes was the Bank Holiday of 1933, which halted the implosion of the banking system. Public assistance programs and direct government make-work programs such as the Works Progress Administration (WPA) also made sense in the face of unemployment rates that were above 20 percent. This is the sort of direct action the electorate no doubt expected in 2009.

Instead, the Democrats seemed to have gambled that the financial crisis would cause the public to welcome a vast extension of the federal government's size and scope, just as the 1930s crisis had done. The result was a year-long, bruising fight over expanding the already extensive federal government control over the health care industry, or more accurately health insurance. This legislation had no connection to the immediate crisis, but had been a party political objective since the 1940s. Jamming through an unwieldy healthcare bill with the slimmest of majorities, and only by stretching parliamentary rules, proved a Pyrrhic victory. The public also proved skeptical of stimulus spending as well as targeted measures to stimulate the consumer-spending engine, including "cash for clunkers" and tax credits for new home purchases. Above all, the monies collected by the government fell with economic activity and employment while outlays grew due to "automatic stabilizers" such as unemployment insurance and other income support. The upshot was an alarming rise in both the federal government deficit and deficit spending by the states, as well as the government share of GDP that reached levels not seen since the Second World War.

The result was the worst midterm election drubbing ever delivered to a first-term president, as opposition to these policies coalesced around the so-called Tea Party movement. (Roosevelt, by contrast, received no effective check to his policies until 1938, in the wake of the return of high unemployment and the ultimate overreach of his attempt to pack the Supreme Court.) The upshot was that a committed and principled majority in the House of Representatives ensured divided government and policy gridlock until the elections of 2012. Whatever one thinks of the merits of specific policies, profoundly divided government in the face of a continuing economic crisis is a dangerous state of affairs.

Legal Missteps

One of the salient facts of the financial crisis is that is has proven very difficult to establish that any laws were broken by individuals who ran the banks. No important bankers have been sent to prison, and though several have lost considerable wealth and reputation, most remain very rich men even after losing their jobs.

This is unfortunate, because the paranoid style of American politics demands that the whole thing was a plot—bizarre as it is to believe that a bunch of bankers thought they could get rich by blowing up the global economy— and plots need flesh-and-blood villains. The legal destruction of a few Bernie Madoff types might have slaked the public's thirst for revenge. In the absence of a scapegoat to punish, the public wants to punish the banks as institutions. Of course, as in the insane practice of shareholders suing companies they invest in, punishing the banks means attacking the viability of the only institutions that actually hold and transmit deposit money for the rest of society. Few politicians understand any of this and fewer care, and the banks by their own practices and behavior have made themselves irresistible targets.

The first thing that has to happen after a financial meltdown is that banks, which had basically burned through their capital before being rescued by the state, need to make lots of money. They need to rebuild their capital out of earnings before investors feel comfortable buying their shares. And they need to do so safely, since they can't be seen returning to the casino to restore their fortunes. As I said above, the policy of ultra-low interest rates and massive government borrowing built in a chance to make piles of risk-free money for the big banks that play in the bond market. However, treasury and trading are not big sources of profits at the average regional banks, much less the thousands of smaller institutions. With unemployment high and households buried in debt, lending to consumers was too risky, and banks were under pressure from their regulators to tighten standards even as the politicians demanded they lend. Business loan demand was, as noted, anemic. The average bank had one intact profit engine: the core bank functions of taking customer deposits and making payments, a business that had largely shifted from paper checks to credit cards and debit cards. When interest rates are at historic averages, this plain-vanilla business can earn half or more of a bank's operating revenue. This is because the cost of funds in the money market will normally be much higher than what banks have to pay their customers in interest. These services also generate a large amount of fee revenue, mostly from customers who do not leave enough money in the bank to pay their way or who overdraw their accounts.

Customers understandably hate these fees, and consumer advocacy groups have been agitating against them for decades. The public, of course, made no distinction between the type of bank that was manufacturing mortgage securities and the bank they had their checking account with. The crisis put all banks in the dock. And to be fair, the largest retail banks had often been extremely aggressive in finding ways to increase fees when times were good. So, even before the passage of Dodd-Frank, Congress passed legislation (notably the Card Act) to limit the ability of banks to charge for overdrafts on checking accounts, to charge for late payment of credit card bills, and to adjust interest rates to reflect changes in customers' risk profiles. The bank lobby that had beaten back many such attempts in the past was on the ropes politically. Now tens of billions of dollars in fee revenue was no longer available to restore the industry balance sheet.

Once the blood was truly in the water, states' attorney general offices and litigators started coming after the banks from all angles. For example, lawyers went after mortgage-servicing practices that had been in place for decades (so-called robo-signing of documents that were never actually looked at) in order to fight off individual foreclosure actions. This turned into an enormous claim against banks that owned large servicing businesses by state attorney generals acting in concert with federal authorities. The sum sought and eventually settled upon—over $20 billion—bears no resemblance to any demonstrable harm, but was intended to provide a source of funds to "keep people in their homes." This raises a politically impossible-to-ask question: is it really good for financially distressed households to be kept in homes they can't afford? The first requirement for a real estate market to recover is that it "clear"—that is, find a bottom at which qualified purchasers will emerge to pick up bargains. This means that the millions of "homeowners" who have zero or negative equity in the homes (so of course do not in any real sense own them) need to revert to being renters sooner or later. The politics of preventing this are irresistible and self-defeating in equal measure. We can confidently expect decades of litigation against the banking industry, some merited and some meritless, but none of it will make it easier to get a loan or buy a house.

Dodd-Frank

There is no scope in this book to examine in any detail Dodd-Frank, as the 848-page Wall Street Reform and Consumer Protection Act is known. This mammoth bill contrasts with the three great financial reform acts of US history: the National Bank Act of 1864, which created national banks and the greenback (29 pages); the Federal Reserve Act of 1913 (32 pages); and of course Glass-Steagall in 1933 (37 pages). Each of these acts defined what financial institutions could and could not do, and in some cases created entirely new institutions. As pointed out in the article "The Dodd-Frank Act: Too Big Not to Fail" in the February 18, 2012 edition of the *Economist*, Dodd-Frank is very different in scope and structure:

> . . . Notes Jonathan Macey of Yale Law School: "Laws classically provide people with rules. Dodd-Frank is not directed at people. It is an outline directed at bureaucrats and it instructs them to make still more regulations and to create more bureaucracies." Like the Hydra of Greek myth, Dodd-Frank can grow new heads as needed.
>
> Take the transformation of 11 pages of Dodd-Frank into the so-called "Volcker rule."[1] . . . In November four of the five federal agencies charged with enacting this rule jointly put forward a 298-page proposal. . . . It includes 383 explicit questions for firms which, if read closely, break down into 1,420 subquestions. . . .
>
> . . . The fifth federal agency involved, issued its own proposal on proprietary trading on January 17th. That one is 489 pages long.

Dodd-Frank instructs 11 financial regulatory bodies, including three new ones, to write about 400 rules and conduct about 100 studies. Each of these rules is—because American rule-making works this way—the object of a comment period by the industry and other parties, so that thousands of pages will be drafted about each before they reach final form. Each rule is capable of running to scores or even hundreds of pages when completed, and each is subject to hundreds of pages of interpretation. Right now, the deadlines laid out in the law are being missed more often than they are being met (93 are finalized), as many key concepts, such as proprietary trading, are proving impossible to define, and many parts of the bill contradict others. Long story short, we have no clear idea at this point what Dodd-Frank will accomplish for anyone— except lawyers and bureaucrats, who will make livings off of its ambiguities.

What we do know is that Dodd-Frank took no account of the causes of the crisis and took pains to avoid examining the roles of Fannie Mae, Freddie Mac, and federal housing policy in creating the housing bubble. In fact, it was passed six months before the completion of a Congressional inquiry in which the majority party members on the committee issued a highly anti-bank report and the minority party an equally anti-GSE dissent.

A key lesson of the crisis—a point that Bagehot made clear a century and a half ago—is that there must be a lender of last resort with complete discretion to act to stop a panic. Dodd-Frank's morass of inconsistent rule-making may even inhibit the Federal Reserve from executing bailouts. No panic in history has ever been foreseen, and inhibiting the discretion of central banks to pour water on the fire is storing up a future disaster for the world economy. A second key lesson is that banks must be free to fail—something that the crony capitalism of the Great Moderation inhibited until the institutions really became too big and interconnected to fail, turning finance into a one-way bet for the bankers.

Dodd-Frank punts on too-big-to-fail, choosing instead to do the impossible: make finance safe. Its approach to doing this is to proscribe activities that had nothing to do with the crisis, such as proprietary trading, and to bring previously unregulated financial entities into the net even if they pose no systemic risk. The final controversial aspect of Dodd-Frank is the creation of a Consumer Protection Agency with broad powers to prevent undefined "abusive" practices. It is operated within and funded by the Federal Reserve System and is therefore beyond the oversight of future congresses. Obviously, governments around the world strive to protect consumers from sharp practices, but it is highly unusual to shield such a function from political accountability.

Basel III

As noted, the Basel process has always been about bank capital, the first line of defense in a financial crisis. Before the crisis, the so-called Basel II rules (which the United States never fully implemented) tried to more closely tie the capital to the actual risks banks were carrying and their ability to measure and manage them. The crisis showed that "scientific" risk management left a lot to be desired, so it was back to capital, and more of it. Basel III added three new wrinkles to global bank regulatory standards. First, the amount and quality of bank capital required against various risk assets will be gradually increased until, by 2019, banks will have to hold, on average, about three times as much tier-one capital—essentially equity and cash equivalents. Second, the Basel Committee learned from the crisis to appreciate the need for banks dependent on interbank markets to have funding to stay afloat if those markets suddenly dry up. As a result, Basel III requires banks to bolster their liquid asset and cash holding enough to survive such episodes. Finally, the process identified 29 global systemically important financial institutions (GSIFIs) for additional capital requirements and more intense supervision—yet another fudge on too-big-to-fail. While only large and internationally active US banks will fall under Basel III, many GSIFIs are US domiciled. How to reconcile Basel III and Dodd-Frank is yet to be resolved.

The original sin of Basel, zero capital weights on sovereign debt, was left unaddressed in a process that was run, not surprisingly, by central banks—institutions that managed their own nations' sovereign debt.

The European crisis of 2011 and 2012 is in many ways the direct result of Basel capital accords giving absurd risk-based capital weightings (basically zero) to sovereign debt. As a result, European banks typically hold too much of it to survive a wave of sovereign defaults. This fundamental flaw remains unaddressed.

The End of the Euro

In the last chapter, I outlined a movie script that included the possibility of a series of sovereign debt crises triggering a second wave of the global financial crisis, with the US financial system taking a body blow in the process. The headlines about the attempts of the European Union to prevent Greece from defaulting on its sovereign debt and possibly starting a domino effect among other euro zone countries have been swinging from hope to despair for three years now, and few Americans outside finance are paying attention. They should. A European financial crisis will at a minimum derail any hope for a US economic recovery and impact China and the other developing markets in ways that inhibit our ability to export. The problem is that there seems to be no good options available to the Europeans, and America is in no position to help. All this is discussed further in Chapter 5, but here it is important to keep in mind the risks the European crisis poses to the US economy.

The intractable dilemma facing the European Union is that Greece can only get out from an unsustainable debt load (itself a product of the euro allowing badly managed countries to borrow as if they were Germany) by defaulting on its obligations in some shape or form. It represents 2 percent of European GDP, so this shouldn't matter, except for the damage it will cause to the balance sheets of French and other continental banks holding Greek bonds. Worse, the other so-called PIIGS (Portugal, Italy, Ireland, Greece, and Spain) have unsustainable public debt as well, and their banks are stuffed with potentially questionable government paper. So the point of bailing out countries is really to prevent a meltdown of the whole European banking sector, something that would roil the global financial system that is still on life support.

Who is providing the life support? The answer is governments with unsustainable public finances.

The EU was in its design never capable of supporting a currency without a fiscal union, meaning a community-wide budget that in turn requires a fully pooled sovereignty capable of direct taxation. A European Central Bank was established and proved to be very credible at monetary policy, but is not and does not want to be a lender of last resort, the one really essential role in a crisis of confidence. The euro, if not the broader European project, may eventually succumb to this fundamental design flaw.

Before the euro even came into effect, the economist Bernard Connolly published *The Rotten Heart of Europe* (Faber & Faber, 1997), a brilliant exposition of the euro as an attempt to force fiscal unification of the EU—a notion that had limited democratic support in member states—through the back door as a necessary response to a crisis like the current one. He has developed several scenarios for the outcome of the current crisis, none very attractive. For example, it may be the Germans who exit, leaving the euro a poor-man's club.

Recently, the very capable governor of the European Central Bank, Mario Draghi, made a bold bet by providing hundreds of billions in euros for three years to EU banks, thus preventing a liquidity crisis in European banking for at least a while. Let's hope it works. Given the deeply interconnected nature of the interbank funding markets, US banks—especially those most beaten down by the first wave of the crisis—are at risk if a wave of sovereign defaults and bank failures rolls over Europe. German and other continental banking systems are even more at risk and less well capitalized. This means that the only proper solution would be some sort of national or even pan-European or transatlantic mega-bailout (something like the 1992 Swedish bank resolution on a global scale). But there is no domestic or international political or legal mechanism to carry out and sustain such an operation. Nor is it possible to believe that it could survive democratic electorates. The German taxpayers and the Tea Party in the US have strong opinions on bailing out the feckless. The banker's greed post-Lehman has reinforced this. The only thing that might fly would be wiping out current management, shareholders, and even most bondholders, while shielding retail deposits. (Some think this actually should have been enacted instead of TARP in 2008–2009, though the politics were impossible at the time.)

This means that the only way out is probably "going Japanese," with governments muddling through by cobbling together rescues and impossible-to-manage mega-banks and keeping them in a regulatory straightjacket while they slowly die of toxic assets. Japan went from 11 so-called city banks and 3 or 4 large trust companies down to 3 gigantic banks, folding in many regional and cooperative banks and the whole finance company sector in the process. The result is a zombie banking system that does not support economic growth and innovation. But it is safe.

In the next chapter, I turn to the unintended economic consequences of attempts to render the world of finance safe.

The Economic Consequences of Financial Regulation

Main Street Caught in the Crossfire

The dividing line between Main Street and Wall Street is nonsense in an economy that has become so heavily finance driven as that of the United States. It feels good to punish the banks, but it always involves punishing ourselves. Accountability for individual bankers is a horse of a different color, and it remains sorely lacking, to be sure. Cutting finance down to size begs the question of what will replace it as a driver of employment and economic growth.

Since the crisis broke, public policy has alternated between attempts to reinflate the credit bubble, especially the housing finance machine, and efforts to rein in finance and effectively turn banking into a public utility. The former includes engineering rock-bottom interest rates, flooding the banks with cheap funds, and blowing up the central bank's balance sheets with purchases of mortgage-related assets and government bonds. (Not only the Fed is playing this game, but central banks in many other countries as well.) These policies, however, have not restored the flow of credit in the Main Street economy, but have mainly resulted in banks hoarding cash in central bank reserve accounts rather than restarting the lending pump.

Another, subtler way of priming the pump has been to reinflate the value of the stock market by reducing the interest on cash deposits and government bonds to rates of return that literally force investors to accept the risks of investing in equities. None of this has made it easier for small businesses or would-be homeowners to actually secure credit, since lending standards were tightened even as rates were locked down. Meanwhile, those depending on interest income have had their spending power slashed to the bone.

Efforts to return banking to its roots as a "public utility" range from an increasing number of state attorney generals and litigators alleging predatory lending (or its opposite, lending discrimination, since banks can be attacked for both). There are also initiatives to set the price of basic services and otherwise expand oversight of the consumer side of the business, notably the Consumer Financial Protection Bureau established under Dodd-Frank, with Harvard Law School professor Elizabeth Warren as a leading advocate. However, it is on the wholesale side of the business that efforts to force a return to utility-style banking may have the largest impacts on Main Street, even if they are indirect. Basically, banking is becoming a less and less attractive place for investors to put money. Interestingly, the FDIC reported in March 2012 that last year not a single de novo bank was chartered in the United States—the first time this has happened in decades. Small banks are continuing to disappear: 140 in 2009, 157 in 2010, and 92 in 2011. As it becomes harder for banks to make money with their own balance sheets and trading books, and as banks face far higher regulatory, capital, and litigation costs, they are either going to pass those burdens on to Main Street in the form of higher prices and less service or simply exit whole market segments.

The general public and politicians seem to believe that providing basic financial services to consumers is very profitable and that banks have been gouging the little guy for years. Even some bank advertising takes this line. The truth of the matter is that providing these services is very expensive—on average as much as $350 per account. Overall deposit and related payment services account for the vast majority of bank costs, especially when you factor in regulatory compliance and fraud losses. Banks had largely been heavily subsidized by a few very profitable consumer businesses, notably mortgage origination and credit card lending, which themselves have incurred heavy losses since the crash. Unless banks can make a competitive return on the higher capital they are being required to keep, the market will simply not give them the capital, forcing them to shrink (as they are already doing in fact, with tens of thousands of layoffs and more to come) and defund low-return businesses such as branch banking. When the bubble was going strong, banks were making major investments in brick-and-mortar Main Street branches, creating jobs and real estate income. This can all go away very quickly.

Distortion of Bank P & Ls and Balance Sheets

Banking is often viewed by the uninformed as the very model and engine of capitalism, which is why critics of capitalism choose to occupy Wall Street and the City of London. Actually, banking has always been in many ways a creature of government and politics. Capitalism demands what the great Austrian economist Josef Schumpeter called "creative destruction." When markets decide which firms deserve money and which don't, the latter will fail; and along with the failure of firms, whole communities and thousands of workers may suffer real hardship. However, by trial and error, markets will tend to give capital to new, innovative companies, such as Apple, and take it away from companies with no future, such as GM. People want iPads and don't want Chevy Volts. This capital allocation by markets has historically been a key economic strength of the United States; the birth and death of companies is far less welcome in more conservative societies such as Europe or Japan, much less socialist economies in which the government allocates capital. Even here, though, democratic politics is not really a friend of market capitalism, because voters understandably crave the economic security that dynamic market capitalism cannot provide them, and elected leaders must promise it to them even if they know better. However, the bottom line is that the freedom to fail is essential to free-market capitalism.

Banks are different. When a company that makes things goes bust, the damage is limited to its owners, employees, and suppliers. Usually they can recoup their losses with new investments, jobs, and customers. When a bank goes bust, even a relatively small one, it can undermine confidence in all banks. This can trigger a run on the banks, with depositors demanding their cash, and set off a full-blown panic leading to a collapse of economic activity on Main Street. Banks, in other words, are the one type of business that can blow up the economy overnight.

This is why, except for a few free-market fundamentalists such as Ron Paul, most sober people recognize a legitimate government interest in licensing and regulating banking companies, although the style and degree of regulation may vary greatly between jurisdictions and over time. It is also why almost all countries have established a central bank—essentially a super-bank that holds the reserves of the banking system, issues the currency, and creates money at will to bail out banks in an emergency. This lender-of-last-resort function is fundamental to central banking, but creates great risks to the taxpayer, so it logically requires that the central bank have an ability to supervise the behavior of private-sector banks. Otherwise, the very fact that someone is willing and able to bail them out of the consequences of risky behavior in fact provides incentives to the private-sector banks for that behavior—a concept knows as a moral hazard, as mentioned previously.

The second key reason why some degree of financial regulation is legitimate is that deposit money in banks forms the basis of the payments system. *Payments system* is an arcane term for all the institutions and mechanisms that allow one person or organization to transfer monetary claims to another. Wire transfers, checks, and plastic cards all play a role in the payments system, as does paper money. There are many parties involved, including consumers, merchants, utilities and other billers, and key infrastructure such as ATM switches and clearinghouses. At the end of the day, however, only banks can really settle financial claims by making one customer's deposit money claim another customer's deposit money claim. Cash, essentially a claim on the government, is the one exception to this in that it can in principle circulate from hand to hand outside the banking system. But while it makes up something like 85 percent of all payments worldwide, it represents a very small percentage of the value exchanged—5 percent or less in some countries. Compared to bank deposit money, it is a rounding error.

Your deposit money claim is the balance in your checking account. When you swipe your debit card, it is reduced by the amount of the transaction, and the party you paid has its claim increased by the same amount. If you and the person you paid are in different banks, they settle up with each other through a clearinghouse or transaction switch, but the final settlement of the claims between the banks only takes place on the books of the central bank. In other words, the banking system is ultimately a big spreadsheet or ledger on computers recording numbers representing the claims on deposit money which everyone in society owns at a given point in time. The payments system moves these blips of data around within a given banking system and also between banking systems worldwide. It is one of those things, such as power and electric light, that we take for granted until they fail to go on when we flick the switch. The government has an interest in seeing that doesn't happen because commerce on Main Street would grind to a halt instantly if the payments system ceased to function.

The regulation of deposit taking and the regulation of payments systems are deeply intertwined. Customarily, even in the absence of a specific law, having an account on the central bank books more or less defines who is a bank. That gives central banks the power to decide the minimum qualifications to be a bank and what activities a bank can engage in. Direct regulation of payments systems has not historically been thought necessary, and fundamentally remains unnecessary, as long as the various private clearinghouses and payments networks are only open to properly licensed and regulated banks. Even before central banking, access to the clearinghouse in any market was a requirement for running a banking business. In a payments clearing, every participant depends on every other participant to pay the house what they owe. That means keeping membership confined to strong, well-managed banks is in the interest of all participants.

Having stipulated that there is a valid public interest in regulating the core, related bank functions of deposit taking and, indirectly, access to the payments system, the real question is how should it be done—though even a bad system of regulation can be executed well by talented people, and the best system is useless without them. The worst of all possible worlds is bad or contradictory rules and regulations and bad execution in compliance and enforcement. That is precisely the risk that overly complicated and prescriptive bureaucratic regulation like that created by Dodd-Frank poses. Let's take a closer look at why.

Supervision vs. Rule Making

Before the crisis broke in 2008, there was a lively debate between banking authorities over "rules-based" vs. "principles-based" regulation, with the United States as poster child for the first and the United Kingdom for the second.

The great virtue of the rules-based approach is that the discretion of the regulator is bounded by a well-drafted rule. If a bank ticks the boxes required and stays inside the foul lines created by the rule, it is "in compliance," and that is that. The weakness of such an approach is that a great deal of mischief can be done by players who can finesse the rules, which are almost always drafted by lawyers, not market participants, and therefore are based on existing instruments, transactions, and identified risks. Rules are always responding to yesterday's accident, so the rule-makers and enforcers are always driving using a rearview mirror. Market players, by contrast, are always scanning the horizon for new opportunities and can find gaps in almost any set of rules, especially if they or their regulatory counsel employ the lawyers who wrote the rules in the first place, which of course they do. A second objection to a rules-based approach is that it quickly becomes a mechanical exercise of box-ticking by regulatory compliance departments staffed by specialists.

The great virtue of a principles-based approach is that broad principles of prudence and fair dealing can be designed to cover almost all future circumstances. The issue is not whether the boxes are ticked, but whether a practice or transaction conforms to well-known principles of acceptable financial conduct, such as prudence and a duty to protect the interests of customers. This of course requires business judgment, not box-ticking, and is less likely to be relegated to compliance departments. Such an approach requires fine judgments and can at times become arbitrary.

In the wake of the crisis, it is hard to maintain that either approach was terribly successful, because very little of what went wrong violated either rules or principles then in force. Bad judgment and plain-old fraud were more at fault. Sometimes, it is useful to remember that the United Kingdom was for centuries the world's leading financial power and London the home of global finance capital without benefit of any formal regulation of either type. Instead, the United Kingdom had a culture in which unwritten rules of fair dealing, a certain clubby self-interested constraint, and informal but strong sanctions for bad behavior sufficed. In this scheme, short of common law crimes such as theft and fraud, the essentially arbitrary judgment of the Bank of England was sufficient to enforce good order. The Bank, which was a private joint-stock company up until 1946, had no legal authority over the market, but it did hold the reserves of the banking system and issue the currency in England and Wales. Access to its discount window and credit could be withheld from banks that in its judgment were doing things that were dangerous or unwholesome for the market.

When exchange control came into force in 1939, the Bank had in its sole discretion the right to extend or withdraw a foreign exchange license, the equivalent of a death sentence for banks. Only after the end of exchange control in 1979 was it felt necessary to establish a formal system of regulation presided over by an independent organization—the Financial Services Authority (FSA)—in place of the Bank. This was part of the sweeping series of reforms called Big Bang that came into force in 1986. The old clubby culture of the City of London quickly collapsed as American institutions and practices took over much of UK banking. As a result, the UK financial system balance sheet grew to over five times GDP and came to drive the entire economy, especially greater London. In the wake of the 2008 crisis, which required two trillion-pound banking groups to be bailed out by the government, it is hard to believe that this was a good bargain for the UK taxpayer.

The Shell Game

The vast expansion of both rules- and principles-based regulation at the expense of the subtler supervision of the markets and players by the Bank of England and its peers set off a game called *regulatory arbitrage*. At its crudest, this simply meant moving the legal locus of activities to the least-regulated jurisdictions, such as the Cayman Islands. However, there were clear limits to this. The more common practice was to game capital adequacy rules—both Basel standards and those set by national regulators. The most straightforward way of doing this was described in the last chapter, as banks put more and more emphasis on mortgages and trading activities among themselves. The development that probably caused the most damage was the asset-securitization process, in which loans were bundled, repackaged, and sold into the capital markets as securities. The mechanics of this are briefly described in my book *Financial Market Meltdown*, but suffice it here to say that asset securitization created a gap between the originator of a loan and its ultimate owner that provided no incentives for bankerly prudence. Moreover, the machinery of asset securitization, the sausage factory, had too many middlemen and rent seekers, all with no particular interest in the underlying credit and a great deal of interest in maximizing their fees.

Probably the most talked-about instance of conflicted interest in the securitization process is the fact that the credit-rating agencies that blessed complex asset-based securities were paid by banks seeking a rating, not by the investors in these securities, as had been the case when these firms started out rating commercial paper. This does not mean they were not honest in their judgments. I know from experience in consulting that they were quite rigorous in their financial modeling, which included scenarios that replicated the Great Depression. No, the problem was simply that the would-be issuer could work with the rating agencies to add layers of insurance and other bells and whistles to the structure of the proposed security until it passed muster. Credit insurers, consultants, lawyers, and bankers all took part in the plastic surgery that turned subprime loans into Triple A securities, and all were to some degree conflicted. What is often forgotten, however, is that throughout the Great Moderation, institutional investors from mutual funds to college endowments were clamoring for high-yielding debt to buy. It should also be remembered this was all possible within the rules-based regulation of the most heavily regulated market on earth.

The expectations of investors and the fact that bank CEOs were rewarded on achieving high returns on equity led banks to alter the mix of their activities to a point where Adair (now Lord) Turner of the FSA said in a speech, "a significant proportion of the activities of the investment and banking industries had no useful social purpose"—a credible assessment coming from a former Chase banker and senior McKinsey consultant to banks. If the purpose of banking is to maximize return on capital, and the Basel Committee and national regulators set standards that can be gamed, basic banking goes out the window because it is simply not a high return-on-equity business in competitive markets. Basic banking is the dull but steady business of taking customer deposits, providing working capital to commerce and industry through short term, self-liquidating loans, and above all providing a payment system. Basic banking was also relationship banking, where the bank manager in the branch or the owner of the community bank know the character and fortunes of their customers, not just a credit score. Once, as Niall Ferguson relates in his underappreciated recent biography of the great Sigmund Warburg, even investment banking was relationship banking. The problem is, of course, that all these things are expensive and, given the high risk-weighting given to business lending, capital intensive. They are also essentially why banks came into being in the first place, and why society has learned to live with them and on occasion save them from themselves.

What regulatory distortions and skewed management incentives both promoted were consumer products that could be securitized, especially mortgages, home equity lines, car loans, and of course credit card receivables. Banking did not really do any of this business before the 1980s, but by the early 2000s it did little but those activities. By then, commercial and industrial loans were less than a fifth of bank assets, and represented an even smaller share of profits, which were driven by a combination of the high margins and high fees associated with retail banking. In reality, it can be argued that banks ceased to be banks and lost the skills and institutional memory to do the lending to Main Street business that used to be their bread and butter. Instead, they took their lead from retailing, turning branches into "stores" and incenting sales associates for selling "products" in place of paying bankers who knew their customers. They expanded their range of products to capture more of the customer wallet through cross-sell strategies, such as giving sales goals and incentives to customer-facing staff to push specific products at anyone they interacted with. Above all, they sought to grow their fee-based revenue and, for the large banks, their treasury and trading profits.

This is not to say that regulation was responsible for these developments; other banking systems responded to Basel capital requirements differently, but it helped make aggressive expansion of a product-focused retail banking culture the path of least resistance. Perhaps more serious, and certainly close to the causes of the 2008 crisis, it favored a high-turnover, "transactional" model of wholesale banking in place of a world where market participants had to know their customers and counterparties. The globalization of capital markets and the wonder of electronic trading systems simply made it too easy to do business in financial assets with little knowledge of their risks.

Have the proposed regulations of Basel III or the Dodd-Frank Act really addressed these distorted incentives? It is hard to see how raising capital requirements encourages a return to basic banking. The notion that credit originators should retain some skin in the game while securitizing loans is appealing, but may prove impossible to implement in practice.

In 2010, the Federal Reserve Bank of New York posted a working paper on its web site that put a size on how large the "shadow banking system"—driven by securitization and market-based funding by hedge funds, institutional investors, and lending from commercial banks—had become on the eve of the 2008 crisis. The number is $20 trillion, at a time when the regulated banking system was only $13 trillion and the GDP about $14 trillion. Congress and the regulatory world worry about this vast source of financing—which has shrunk since the crisis, but is still probably larger than the "official" banking system—and the Fed did in the event have to prop it up to a degree during the panic. Since the shadow banking system has no access to the Federal Reserve discount window or federal deposit insurance, and is outside the payments system, its players can and do fail. Their investors lose money. Dodd-Frank and regulators in Europe would like to bring the shadow banking system within the same regulatory restraints that motivated its creation in the first place. The real question might be, Why isn't more finance subject to real free-market creative destruction?

One thing we can be sure of is that the era of expanding access to credit and financial services—what has sometimes been called the retail banking revolution—is over, at least in the developed economies.

Restriction of Financial Access

When the first joint-stock banks (banks owned by shareholders) emerged in the United Kingdom nearly two centuries ago, the established banks were all private partnerships with unlimited liability (the one exception being the Bank of England, which was as a government-backed monopolist a de facto enemy of the privately owned banks and kept out of the clearinghouse). The joint-stock banks were also shunned by the clearinghouse run by the private banks, given their shocking business model: they opened branches where the general public, not just rich City of London merchants and brokers, could open accounts and make payments using checks. The fact that they were public companies allowed them to raise the capital needed to convince the public their money would be safe without unlimited liability and, of course, to put up branches on every British High Street. The business proved insanely profitable by the estimates that Bagehot gave in *Lombard Street*, but banks were very choosy about who was a suitable customer, and they required substantial sums to open an account (the equivalent of three or four years income for the average UK subject). Despite this, the model of branch banking spread around the world and gave the fast-growing middle and professional classes access to convenient payments, savings, and credit. This population was "banked," a sort of economic enfranchisement that their fellow citizens did not qualify for.

The consumer culture of the United States and other high-income Western countries has been much maligned by some intellectuals, but as Ferguson points out in *Civilization: The West and the Rest* (Penguin, 2011), it is a "killer app" that has made the West extraordinarily successful in material terms. A "banked" population is absolutely foundational to a vibrant consumer culture. Economic historians have traced the spread of white bread, once largely restricted to the upper classes in Britain and France, in society and across Europe as people became more prosperous in the late 18th and 19th centuries.

A similar "white bread line" can be traced in access to banking. Most advanced was the white bread–eating USA, where it was widely felt that everyone should have access to the same services and conveniences. By the early 1950s, at least half the population had a financial account that could be used for payments, the bedrock definition of being banked. Being paid in cash became rare, as most companies adopted paychecks. Once people became used to cashing checks, they became more inclined to open checking accounts and paying their bills by mailing checks. The banked US population probably peaked in the 1990s at around 85 percent of households. The countries of continental Europe, or more precisely the northern European states and France, began to mandate that employees be paid directly into financial accounts. A bank account essentially became a routine condition of employment. An increasing number of services and utilities came to require or at least forcefully push mandates that allowed them to be paid automatically out of these accounts. The United Kingdom stood somewhere in the middle, with perhaps as little as 20 percent of the population properly banked in the 1960s, but up to and above American levels by the 1990s.

Now, it is possible to make a case, as historian Louis Hyman does well in *Debtor Nation* (Princeton University Press, 2011), for a view that almost universal access to finance led to abusive practices and helped addict the American consumer to credit. Most development economists, however, would support the view that access to finance helps drive economic growth, social inclusion, and rising living standards. The balance of regulatory and political thinking before the crisis was on the side of maximizing financial inclusion, and the

World Bank and other national and multilateral development agencies made it a priority. Now, for better or worse, the pendulum has swung sharply in the opposite direction in the developed world.

There is often a presumption by well-meaning politicians and reformers that all businesses are predatory and all customers are victims if not protected by government paternalism. Private enterprise shouldn't necessarily be abolished, but needs to be directed by government to some higher good than profits and growth. An example of this impulse to pursue social justice through regulation of industry is the Community Reinvestment Act (CRA), passed in 1977 at the height of the Jimmy Carter era of stagflation and disillusionment with government programs. The CRA was an ingenious way of empowering community activists and social reform groups to seek lending commitments to "underserved" communities, which in America were largely concentrated among racial minorities in the inner city. As expanded by subsequent legislation, the CRA required the Federal Reserve and other financial regulators to grant permissions for actions such as mergers, branch closures, expansions, and the like only to banks that had a satisfactory CRA rating. Community activists and "community organizers" such as the Association of Community Organizers for Reform Now (ACORN) not only had direct input into the process, but could orchestrate boycotts and demonstrations that few bankers were willing to stand up to, so the CRA proved potent at siphoning off shareholders' funds into political activism. It also made some prominent activists rich and powerful.

Now, we should not overestimate the CRA's influence. The banking industry and the regulators learned to live with it. However, it reflected a widespread notion that is almost uniquely American: that every citizen is entitled to credit and other banking services. In a homogeneous and wealthy society such as Sweden, this would be harmless. But in a radically unequal and diverse society such as the United States, it would have been fatal within a traditional banking model. To make credit judgments based on knowledge of people's character and circumstances would run afoul of the plethora of laws and court decisions seeking to ban racial and other forms of discrimination. Credit judgments are by nature a form of discrimination between good credit risks and bad credit risks. Also, since banks only make money from people who have money, the very premise that they were serving communities rather than individuals and businesses meant that the CRA was just another tax—a cost of doing business.

What made the notion of a fundamental right to credit downright dangerous was the very business that eventually caused the 2008 crisis, subprime lending. For centuries, banks turned away all but the most creditworthy borrowers because bad loans could easily bring them down. Their shareholders' capital, as well as their depositors' money, was always at risk. Loan securitization changed all that. Banks learned how to package and sell off their loans. If a bank has no skin in the game, it can extend credit to liars, thieves, and deadbeats—even pets and dead people. Asset securitization took the skin out of the game. The subprime mortgage market involved lenders who created structures that required very low or no down payment, almost no documentation of assets or income, and very low initial rates of interest. This business was profitable as long as the sausage factory was humming, and was largely guaranteed and encouraged by the GSEs and their congressional patrons, notably Messrs. Dodd and Frank. In other words, the miracle of scientific financial engineering produced housing credit for all, and fat profits for everyone in the housing food chain, plus the political advantages of increasing home ownership among the less well-to-do, something that political conservatives embraced as "the ownership society." The CRA might have been the catalyst, but the profit motive and political calculation produced the chain reaction that drove the bubble.

The expansion of two other key aspects of financial inclusion also reflected innovation by banks rather than government mandates. The most important was the development of highly sophisticated predictive models that allowed credit card issuers to profitably expand into the subprime, or non-creditworthy, segments. These models allowed them to accurately forecast default rates. It also helped them set interest rates and penalty fees according to both initial underwriting risk and behaviors that caused that risk to shoot up, such as missing payments or making late payments on almost any bill. Since banks were free to set initial rates and boost them, as well as apply penalty fees based on actual customer behavior, a much higher proportion of the populace enjoyed access to consumer credit (as opposed to loan sharks and pawn shops, the traditional resort of the unbanked) than in other societies and at any other time in our history.

The second important development was the substantial expansion of free checking, with very moderate balance requirements, as well as rewards programs offering benefits such as airline miles for using payment cards and other products. These incentives mainly reflected the intensely competitive nature of mass-market retail banking. However, as noted, maintaining a transaction account involves substantial expenses, from regulatory overhead to brick-and-mortar branches. Rewards also need cash income to fund them. In both cases, the offset came from collecting fees—for bounced checks and overdrafts from checking customers who failed to manage their accounts carefully, and for transactions involving "premium" or reward cards from merchants. These fees funded things that many consumers wanted and would pick a bank or credit card because of, but obviously the people paying them were less than happy.

In the juncture of finance and politics, no good deed goes unpunished. Consumer advocates, politicians, and lawyers all developed grievances against the institutions that had provided access to finance, choice, and differentiated value propositions on an unprecedented scale.

Consumer Protection vs. Access

There is no doubt that retail banks took an aggressive stance in expanding their subprime businesses and maximizing fee revenue. Banks did in fact maximize the number of overdrafts through manipulating the order in which debts and credits to accounts were posted, and charged penalties on bounced checks that were perhaps in excess of the direct cost of handling them. However, nobody was forced to open a free checking account, or for that matter to bounce checks. The high rates charged for subprime credit reflected real risk, a fact supported by ample statistics.

Consumer advocates would of course characterize many retail banking industry practices as predatory, and with some justice. In retrospect, banks were doing themselves no favors by expanding into and then growing dependent on consumer financial services, especially to the less affluent and creditworthy segments of the population. The basic banking model assumed that the main function of commercial banks was, well, commercial lending. Few politicians or social reformers assume that businesses can't look out for themselves, except perhaps small businesses, which have been objects of political largesse for decades. Consumers can be presented as perpetual victims of the banks or, for that matter, any corporation providing a product or service.

For example, one of the standard accusations against banks before the CRA was *redlining*: the exclusion of low-income or minority neighborhoods from mortgage or other credit. Banks and insurers had in fact engaged in such practices before Congress acted to ban them. However, when banks expanded into the subprime markets in the previously redlined demographic, they opened themselves to charges of predatory lending from the same quarters that once accused them of discrimination. The only way to avoid this dilemma in the United States is to avoid involvement in retail banking completely. But once the surviving Wall Street investment banks became bank-holding companies to qualify for Federal Reserve support, they too fell under the CRA. As noted, the crisis has empowered the adversaries of the banks to impose sweeping changes in the way banks deal with consumers. For example, under the so-called Card Act (which predates Dodd-Frank), banks cannot change the terms of a customer's credit card loan as long as they are current on their payments. This mean that banks cannot price for risky behavior, which in turn forces them to narrow the band of people they will underwrite in the first place. With risk-based pricing out the window, banks will have no choice but to increase the cost of credit to everyone. Ending or curtailing a bank's ability to extract overdraft fees and capping what they can charge merchants for debit card transactions will make tens of millions of consumer accounts unremunerative. This has already made it difficult to fund popular rewards programs. The new, and by design, unaccountable, Consumer Protection Agency is almost certain to make things much worse for retail financial services. The agency will potentially have power to essentially dictate the design of consumer financial products, their pricing, and how they are sold. No matter how the balance of political power shifts, it is hard to see any political capital to be gained in defending the freedom of retail banks to make a profit. Equally, it may be impossible for banks to justify committing capital to the consumer sector under such restrictions.

The End of Product Differentiation

One of the great triumphs of information technology was the defeat of *Fordism*, the industrial logic that since it is more efficient to produce standard products, everyone gets the same thing: the consumer can have any car as long as it is black. Information technology, especially in service industries, allows almost infinite customization to the needs and preference of individuals. For example, there are web sites that allow consumers to design their own credit cards, trading off factors such as interest rate, credit limit, rewards, and other features. The vision of a "market of one" is increasingly achievable, with consumers co-designing or even dictating what they are willing to pay for and what trade-offs they are willing to make. This of course assumes a basic level of savvy among most consumers, and their basic capacity to consult their own interest and preferences and make rational choices. Of course, to admit such a thing is to refute a key tenet of the consumer protection movement, and indeed, the entire rationale for the modern regulatory state.

Clearly, to protect people from the predatory nature of bankers, only a few simple and standard products should be permitted, with simple and standard pricing. Elizabeth Warren, who created the basic structure of the Consumer Finance Protection Bureau (CFPB) before departing to run for Senate, is on record in support of such an approach. This is from the journal *Democracy* (issue 5, summer 2007):

So why not create a Financial Product Safety Commission (FPSC)? Like its counterpart for ordinary consumer products, this agency would be charged with responsibility to establish guidelines for consumer disclosure, collect and report data about the uses of different financial products, review new financial products for safety, and require modification of dangerous products before they can be marketed to the public. The agency could review mortgages, credit cards, car loans, and a number of other financial products, such as life insurance and annuity contracts. In effect, the FPSC would evaluate these products to eliminate the hidden tricks and traps that make some of them far more dangerous than others.

This assumes, among other things, that the financial services that people require are already set in their forms and functions, such as toasters and other appliances that are governed by consumer safety legislation. They are not. Financial technology is (or at least was before the crisis) advancing rapidly by trial and error, so prescribing what a safe and fair product would constitute would really require a sort of financial Food and Drug Administration (FDA) to test and approve innovative products. The FDA stands accused of inhibiting medical innovation, but is weighted with the issues of life and health in its care. However, it also benefits from a scientific methodology. In consumer financial services there is neither that risk nor that benefit since potential harm and objective measurement are less obvious. My fear is that, intended or not, active and intrusive consumer protection of the sort the industry seems likely be exposed to will more or less compel the end of financial innovation by banks who will seek shelter in standard government-approved products. Creators of new services outside the regulated financial services arena—essentially the Googles and PayPals of this world—may continue to attract capital and grow, but the banks themselves are unlikely to recover the costs of any service innovations they develop.

In *Financial Market Meltdown*, I expressed considerable skepticism abut the value or soundness of financial innovation, taking my lead from Bagehot, who said that the ways of lending money safely are few in number, easily learned, and admit of no variation. However, that really applied to wholesale market innovations that allowed credit to be turned into bonds through complex financial alchemy. Retail consumer products and services are going through a period of rapid and discontinuous change driven by the Internet and mobile communications. Many of the most promising concepts are being developed outside the regulated banks. Inhibiting banks from investing in this revolution will not halt progress entirely, but it will keep much of it in unregulated corners of the universe. Nowhere is this truer than in the critical arena of consumer payments.

Unbanking the Banked

For a high-income industrial society, America already has a staggering number of unbanked or underbanked households, estimated by the FDIC at a quarter of the total economically active population. Some of this reflects the high level of recent immigration, legal and undocumented, and the number of households living below the poverty line—both factors that set America apart from other rich countries and always has. Some of it reflects the suspicion of banks, much of it deserved, felt by many people without much money or education. We stand at the cusp of a much cheaper and more transparent consumer financial services model based on mobile devices. Poor countries such as Kenya have already demonstrated the potential of mobile money to improve the lives of people living on a few dollars a day. These same technologies and business models could vastly increase financial inclusion in the United States. However, the rush of post-crisis legislation—including the Card Act discussed previously; the Durbin Amendment to Dodd-Frank, which sets prices on debit card transactions; and above all, the establishment of an unaccountable CFPB with expansive powers under Dodd-Frank—could swing the pendulum in the direction of reducing the incentives of banks to operate in the consumer segment. With the two critical income streams—overdraft fees and interchange fees of debit card transactions—that permitted banks to defray the cost of providing a transaction account to middle-income and low-income households being slashed or capped by regulatory fiat, tens of millions of accounts will become hopelessly unprofitable for banks to maintain. However, the public will blame the banks, not the politicians, when free checking disappears and the price of having a bank account goes up. When Bank of America tried to recoup billions in lost debit card revenue resulting from the Durbin Amendment, public outrage forced them to back off on debit card fees. This is not a fight banks can win.

In most countries, the mass market and lower-income consumer is served by the post office, which provides basic account services such as savings and bill payment at a much lower cost than full-service commercial banks. In their wisdom, the New Dealers got the US Postal Service out of the retail banking business in the 1930s in an attempt to divert savings to the building-and-loan, or S&L, business. As a result, the United States is the only important financial market without a postal bank for the bottom income brackets. Congress would never dare try to restore postal banking in the teeth of opposition from community banks and credit unions. Congress's preferred strategy over recent decades has been to try to place a burden on the commercial banks by forcing them to provide "life-line banking," a profitless proposition even before a massive increase in the regulatory burden made serving the mass market even less economic.

Many banks will have no choice but to reduce their investment in retail banking and make their services more expensive. Thirty years ago, my former employer, Manufacturers Hanover, was told by McKinsey that a household in New York City making less than $65,000 a year was unprofitable to serve as a core banking customer. Today that number would be north of $250,000. Banks are kennels for money, and only people with dogs need kennels. They tend to be the "1 percent."

If the banks are more or less forced by politicians and regulators to push the "99 percent," or a large portion of them, out of the system (the bank analyst Meredith Whitney estimates the proportion of unbanked is going up from one in five to two in five), where will they go? As we have seen recently, the credit unions and community banks have a limited ability to absorb them, though they are a good option for many. The big winners are likely to be an increased use of cash, check-cashing services, and payday lenders.

One of the key advantages to banking essentially the whole active population, as most European countries and Japan have managed to do, is that it reduces the role of these informal and often predatory "alternative" financial service providers and the role of cash in everyday transactions. This tends to reduce the size of the informal, or gray, economy. A bank account was once essentially a luxury good until Americans more or less made it a right and the rest of the world followed suit. Now it is widely viewed as a necessity, helping countries develop and grow their economies by helping ordinary people to save, access credit, and pay their bills. America is moving in the opposite direction.

Hurting the Savers and Investors

A central fact in any society is that citizens rely on government to protect them from the theft of their property. When governments take actions that destroy the savings and therefore the retirement income of citizens, their policies—once recognized for what they in fact are—stir the deepest social unrest. The inflation that was the product of the Weimar Republic's efforts to get out from under its debts destroyed the German middle class and led to the nightmare years of the 1930s and 1940s. The Great Inflation that followed the Johnson and Nixon years destroyed perhaps 70 percent of household savings in the United States until halted by Paul Volcker. Once begun, inflation is extremely difficult and painful to halt. Damping down inflation, which everywhere is a matter of creating too much money relative to the output of goods, is a central bank responsibility of the highest order.

After the collapse of a financial bubble, as occurred in the United States in the 1930s and Japan in the 1990s, the more immediate threat is the opposite of inflation. It is deflation, the relentless drop in the price of assets as society responds by trying to pay down debt and save. It was this "liquidity trap" Keynes was trying to cure with his advice to offset private thrift with government spending. However, vast increases in government spending and debt have proven ineffective in halting Japanese deflation. And while the United States has avoided actual deflation, the effects of massive increases in government spending, debt, and the money supply have been remarkably feeble.

At such a juncture, the retirement income and savings of households face a double threat: either the government will deliberately stoke inflation to reduce the real value of the money it must pay back its creditors, or it will try to keep interest rates as low as possible as long as possible so that the interest service on the debt is manageable. The only way out of this dilemma is if economic growth can be revived at a rate where the debt burden shrinks as a percentage of the economy. This does not appear likely given the vast increase in regulation and distortions in the allocation of capital on one hand, and the large overhang of debt that households carry. This debt burden is to a large degree a product of decades of bipartisan government policy to direct capital away from productive investment (high taxation of corporate profits and income from savings and investment) and toward sterile but popular investment in residential housing (mortgage interest deduction, the GSEs, and home-loan banks). As long as it is seen as politically important to keep mortgage interest rates low in order to reinflate the housing market and limit foreclosure, the tens of millions of responsible Americans who saved for retirement will receive almost no income from their investments. This in itself depresses spending and business activity, but it gets worse. Artificially low rates of interest threaten the ability of pension funds at the state and local level to meet trillions of dollars of contractual promises made to government employees for retirement and health care—promises that could not have been met even with historical rates of interest. Private insurance and annuities face similar challenges. It is inconceivable that the gaps can be filled by taxation without further depressing economic growth and the tax base to support future retirees.

Of course, as a reserve currency, the United States has more scope to buy time by printing money and running debt at the federal level than states that are staring into a financial abyss—such as Greece and Italy—potentially bringing down the euro zone as a whole. But several American states, such as California and Illinois, are in equally hopeless positions.

The finance-driven economy of the last quarter-century had many flaws and resulted in a financial panic of epic proportions. But the financial economy was an engine of growth in the real economy that made the burden of government spending and future retirement manageable. Until we manage to restore the broken markets to a functioning growth engine, our future is likely to be bleak indeed. It can be done; we have just been going about it in the wrong way.

The next chapter will explore what life will be like for all of us after cutting finance down to size.

Life After Finance

Living Within One's Means

What will economic life be like for average Americans, or Europeans for that matter, after the policies and regulations discussed in the last chapter take hold? We are going back to the future, to a world where elected and unelected officials, not bankers, are in the economic driver's seat. We do not face Armageddon, but we do face a world of less growth, less opportunity, and less freedom in economic matters. That would not necessarily be a bad trade-off for economic security and stability. The odds are, however, that we won't get that either.

Is Government Spending Like Household Spending?

The state of public finances has understandably been a major focus of the 2012 election cycle in the United States and is at the very center of the European crisis. Common sense tells the average person that they cannot live beyond their income for long. Politicians often compare public finances to good household management, something Margaret Thatcher in the United Kingdom was particularly effective at doing. In the always-simplistic rhetoric of politics, fear-mongering about the size and growth of the public debt is commonplace. It is often couched in the sentimental notion that our kids and grandkids are going to have to pay these debts off someday, and we are doing them real harm.

History suggests that this view is nonsense. Governments are fundamentally different than households. Countries are not mortal in the way individuals are, so they really don't ever have to pay off their debts as long as they can afford to pay interest. And their debts can be perpetual—the British government once actually issued perpetual debt in the form of so-called consuls—as long as they can be rolled over by borrowing new money. The ability to keep borrowing, of course, depends on the confidence of investors that governments will not *default*—a term much used in the debt-ceiling standoff of 2011, but little understood. A formal sovereign default means that a government has ceased to make payments of interest and principle to bondholders. If payments resume, the default is "cured," but many other things can happen that also hurt bondholders, including the consolidation and restructuring of debt. The real reason for investor confidence in government debt is that most other borrowers are a greater risk most of the time. Governments have the ability to take their citizens' money in the form of taxes under penalty of fines or prison. Companies have to actually generate cash by producing and selling goods and services, and households need a paycheck. Which is the safer bet?

The Birth of the Credit-Driven Economy

Rather than being a threat or a menace, a substantial national debt is an essential anchor to a functioning financial market. The whole history of finance is largely a history of public debt. Modern finance was born in the City of London when the British crown needed to refinance an enormous debt mountain, the byproduct of wars to contain France. The ingenious solution was to give a 150-year monopoly on joint-stock banking—a shareholder-owned public bank rather than a bank owned by individuals or a partnership—to a new company called the Bank of England in 1694. The monopoly plus the interest guaranteed by the crown allowed the Bank to buy up the debt with funds provided by investors across Europe. This debt was essentially guaranteed by the taxing powers of the crown. It was "good as gold," and with its backing, the bank could issue its own bank notes and otherwise expand the supply of paper credit. It also kept "managing"—paying interest and principle, and issuing new bonds—the debt mountain it had bought. The mountain kept growing, with Britain and France at war much of the time between 1694 and 1815. By that time, the British public debt stood at 260 percent GDP. Yet, by 1850, the public debt had fallen to 100 percent of GDP, and 30 years later was below

50 percent. Some of this due to the fact that the size and scope of government was very limited everywhere before the Second World War. Long periods of peace allowed governments to cut back, and between 1815 and 1914 Britain was almost constantly at peace. However, it came to be broadly understood in Britain that debt is a form of money (even a dollar bill is a debt the government owes the holder), and that far more trade and industry could be carried on with debt than with cash. The result was the first credit-driven economy. It coincided with what we call the Industrial Revolution, which was not just a series of clever inventions but whole new industries, jobs, and lifestyles. The growth in output stemming from industrial innovation and credit allowed the debt to shrink as a share of the economy over time.

Unlike many of his contemporaries—above all Jefferson and Madison—Alexander Hamilton understood how essential a national debt managed by a central bank was to Britain's economy. His successful efforts to have the federal government of the New Republic assume the national debt and charter a Bank of the United States modeled on the Bank of England were the foundations of the modern American economy. Interestingly, the populist hero Andrew Jackson killed off the Bank of the United States and actually paid off the national debt, with ruinous results for an economy starved of credit. The concept that all money is really debt, not something made by the government or poured from money heaven, is probably no better understood today than in the time of Jackson, the bank slayer. Basically, the debt of a national government is the highest-quality debt, and can be multiplied as it is used as collateral for other debt, such as overnight borrowing between banks. It is the core money in the system, and the notion of paying it off is based on a misunderstanding of what money is and how it works.

How to Keep Interest Rates Low

The issue with public debt is not really how much of it there is in absolute terms, but whether or not the government can afford to pay the interest on it. This in turn largely depends on the rates at which it was contracted originally and the rates at which it can be rolled over into new debt. Japan, for example, has public debt even higher than Britain did in 1815, and unlike Britain has scant chance of growing its economy. However, the cost of money in Japan has been almost zero for decades and is unlikely to rise with a shrinking population and falling prices. The price of money in the long run depends on how much you can make by borrowing it. A slow-growth or shrinking economy makes money cheap, while in a boom optimistic entrepreneurs bid up its price. That is the theory. In fact, the government is such a big player in the post-2008 world, market forces and price signals don't really work. The

Fed has pumped so much money into the banking system—an operation that is often called "printing money" but is really about buying government debt and other assets from banks—that rates of interest on treasury securities are at historic lows. The S&P downgrade of US debt below AAA may have been unprecedented, but it certainly had no real effect on government borrowing costs. Given the state of the world, US government debt is about as safe a place to park money as investors worldwide can hope to find. Demand for safety, the so-called flight to quality, will keep rates on the debt of the United States low as long as the economic prospects of other regions, notably the euro zone, are questionable. Private demand for money will stay subdued until companies and households become convinced that a real recovery is underway. However, something more permanent is afoot: a return to a set of policies that are presented by the government of the United States and other heavily indebted countries as financial system reform and prudent regulation to make finance safe and protect the public from the excesses of the banks— but that really amount to a stealth tax. The formal economic term for this is *financial repression*. The good news is that financial repression works in both making high debt levels affordable and in reducing them over time. The bad news is that it massively redistributes wealth from savers and investors to the government.

Financial Repression Made Simple

In a recent paper for the National Bureau of Economic Research (NBER), *The Liquidation of Government Debt* (NBER Working Paper 16893, March 2011) Carmen Reinhart and M. Belen Sbrancia make the case that between 1945 and the 1970s, almost all advanced countries practiced "a subtle type of debt restructuring," financial repression, to achieve "sharp and rapid" reduction of public debt as a portion of their economies. Financial repression has three key pillars:

 • First, governments directly or indirectly set interest rates that are below what the market would set. From the 1930s to 1982, this was done explicitly with the imposition of caps on how much interest, if any, banks could pay depositors. Today it is done by the Fed's monetary policy, which is essentially very loose. This tends to produce inflation greater than interest rates available to savers most of the time. So-called *negative real interest rates*, where money saved in a bank loses purchasing power, prevailed most of the time from the 1940s up until the 1980s.

- Second, "prudential regulation" (Dodd-Frank is an extreme example but every country regulates finance to one degree or another in the interest of protecting society) of banks, pension funds, and other institutional investors forces them to favor government debt even when it offers lousy returns. Again, in the immediate postwar decades, blunt controls on capital exports and foreign-exchange transactions were widely employed to make this happen. Today, the holding of government debt can be required of banks and institutions in the name of safety and soundness. The impact is the same: as the NBER working paper puts it, "Creation and maintenance of a captive domestic audience that facilitated directed credit to the government" is a key aspect of financial repression.

- The third pillar of repression is structural: the direct government ownership of banks, or effective government direction of their business decisions, including measures to direct credit to government-favored uses. Restrictions on entry into the financial industry and reducing the number of competitors through consolidation are also part of the package.

How does financial repression work? Basically, it sees to it that investors are herded into buying and holding government debt at negative real interest rates while inflation eats away at the real value of the debt. If the combination of low rates and inflation runs to 4 or 5 percent a year, the value of debt as a percentage of the economy can fall 40 or 50 percent in a decade, even without compounding. For example, I noted previously that the United Kingdom ran up debts equal to 260 percent of GDP in order to beat Napoleon, and then took 40 years to get that number below 100 percent. After World War II, UK debt was again over 2.5 times GDP, but was below 100 percent within 20 years.

The United States did equally well in working down its debt after World War II. In all these cases, the growth spurt of the 1950s and 1960s fueled by reconstruction and pent-up demand was a great help. But equally, the lack of economic freedom embodied in wartime controls, as well as the regulatory state created by the New Deal combined with the global rules of the Bretton Woods system made all the difference. The world of the 19th century was characterized by a system of free trade, free markets, and sound, noninflationary money anchored by the gold standard. Countries could not effectively debase their currencies or generate inflation without having to pony up real money: gold. The only way out was either default or a negotiated restructuring with the bondholders, both wrenchingly embarrassing for any country. With a regime of pure fiat currencies—that is, money that is only worth something because the government says it is worth something and the market has to go along—governments can get away with a lot more. Above all, two global wars in which the government exerted a degree of economic control previously unimaginable has made the publics of all advanced economies amenable to accepting a level of regulation and intervention in financial markets that makes financial repression seem normal.

The Rules of Repression

If you think that the vast and open-ended smorgasbord of financial rule-making mandated by Dodd-Frank is not an opening to full-blooded financial repression like that of the postwar era, then you are missing the whole point of the exercise. Under the terms of the current, somewhat naïve political debate, free-market advocates say that getting government off the back of business will allow us to grow our way out from beneath the debt overhang. The "progressive" view is that debt per se is not a problem if taxes are raised on the 1 percent, although they already carry 40 percent or more of the tax burden. As with many such political standoffs, everybody is wrong.

The odds of the US economy growing out of our debt overhang are extremely long if past experience is any guide. Carmen Reinhart and Ken Rogoff studied centuries of financial crises—read their indispensible *This Time Is Different* (Princeton University Press, 2009) for the full picture—and found that public debt levels began to impede economic growth when they moved above 90 percent of GDP. The mean growth drag was 1 percent, and a 1 percent drag on GDP makes a huge difference in the size of an economy over time. To say that we are going to grow our way out of debt when debt is already a significant drag is a bit of a stretch. The old tried-and-true nostrum of tax cuts only accelerates the debt expansion in the short run, though fundamental tax system reform to broaden the base could actually increase revenue and accelerate debt reduction. The problem is of course that fundamental reform of the tax code involves simplification in one form or another, and it is the very complexity of tax provisions that allows the permanent political class in Washington to sell favorable treatment to industry lobbies and other special interests. It is hard to see Congress doing something that takes away a key lever for fund-raising and horse-trading.

Raising—or Lowering—Taxes Has Little Impact

On the other hand, tax cuts such as the payroll tax holiday have no impact on capital formation and savings, activities that are already discouraged by the tax code. Raising taxes on the "rich" would not make a real dent in the debt overhang—100 percent taxation at the top 1 percent would cover half of one year's deficit—but would almost certainly discourage business investment.

As the European crisis of today illustrates, as well as numerous debt crises in other countries that couldn't just print money, if you can't grow and tax your way out of a debt overhang, you are left with two options: default and austerity. Both are very ugly, as the riots in Europe and the public-sector union reaction to minor reforms in the United States should remind us. Public debt before the postwar era was almost entirely the product of war, which along with law and order and diplomacy used to be the only legitimate purpose of national government. After World War II, the notion that the national government had an obligation to provide health, education, and welfare benefits and redistribute income took hold. When half or more of the population depends upon and feels entitled to state largesse, and only a few pay the taxes to provide it, austerity is political suicide, even for nominally conservative parties. Wars end, but entitlements are forever.

And this is the beauty of financial repression. It represents a massive stealth tax on wealth—not just the wealthy—that few people even understand and nobody debates in public. As Reinhart and Sbrancia put it so well in their NBER working paper:

> The financial repression tax has some interesting political-economy properties. Unlike income, consumption, or sales taxes, the "repression" tax rate (or rates) are determined by financial regulations and inflation performance that are opaque to the highly political realm of fiscal measures. Given that deficit reduction usually involves highly unpopular expenditure reductions and (or) tax increases of one form or another, the relatively "stealthier" financial repression tax may be a more politically palatable alternative.

Of course, there are limits to this neat trick of impoverishing the thrifty to feed the government and its dependents by reducing the value and income of savings. Inflation often breaks out suddenly with little or no warning, and can run unchecked as it did in the 1970s during the so-called Great Inflation that wiped out most of the value of American savings in a few years. Then, the so-called bond vigilantes simply refused to buy government debt on the terms offered. Eventually, Regulation Q, which capped interest rates, was abolished as savers abandoned the banking system, and the heroic actions of Paul

Volcker broke the back of inflation by inducing a deep and painful recession. He did that by jacking rates up as high as 20 percent. When the smoke cleared, perhaps as much as 70 percent of the wealth of savers and investors had been liquidated.

Right now, there are voices saying that a little more inflation would be a good thing for the economy, but perhaps because financial repression is firmly in place there is no sign of bond vigilantes riding to the rescue. This would all be bad enough, but the trajectory of public debt is pointing skyward in the developed world. Consider the McKinsey Global Institute analysis "Debt and Deleveraging: The Global Credit Bubble and Its Economic Consequences" (January 2010), as updated in 2011. It shows that total debt in the United States (where, unlike in many countries, private consumer debt is a huge part of the problem) had grown 67 percent between 2000 and 2010, a rate only exceeded by Italy. By contrast, in Germany, where the word for debt—*schuld*—also means "guilt" or "shame," total debt levels are only slightly below those of the United States, but mostly in the public sector and owed to German nationals. The growth in total debt from 2000 to 2010 was only 15 percent. By some estimates, the unfunded liabilities of the US government and its state and local subdivisions—a combination of entitlements and public-sector pensions and health care obligations—are around ten times the size of the economy. This is somewhat misleading because the size of the economy, when the bill comes due, is ultimately decisive in determining what is affordable. That is why unfunded pension plans, such as Social Security in the United States and similar plans in most other advanced countries, have worked up to this point. If worse comes to worst, governments can do what they have done for centuries and change the rules of the game when it becomes necessary. Congress, for example, is under no legal obligation to pay Social Security participants a dime.

The Political Direction of Credit and Investment

In China—an economy much admired by Thomas Friedman of the *New York Times* and Andy Steen, former president of the Service Workers International Union (and a large number of Western corporate leaders as well)—the mechanism of financial repression is in rude health. All banks are owned or controlled by the state. Interest rates on the massive savings of the Chinese pubic are capped at 3 percent or so, while inflation is running at twice that rate or more. The financial repression tax is huge, but in a country where formal taxation is less than efficient at getting the state's "fair share" from entrepreneurs, it at least falls on those with money in the bank. Those banks in turn keep millions employed in state enterprises that would have gone out of existence in a market-driven banking system. They also allow the favored projects and sectors in a planned economy to grow. Of course, there is little or no bank credit for entrepreneurs and start-ups without government connections, much less for consumers. Loan sharks and shadow banks of all sorts meet those needs at very high rates of interest. Overall, though, the banks serve as effective instruments of government policy, able to speed up growth or put the brakes on overheated sectors, such as real estate, on command.

This model of banking as a government-run utility in service of political priorities is not limited to socialist-style planned economies. Postwar Japan, another model of "industrial policy" much admired by many US commentators in the 1980s, had a highly directed and uncompetitive banking system providing low-cost savings to industry. That system also did nothing much for small business or consumers, but, until it blew up in 1990, it produced what were for a time the world's largest and seemingly most solid banks—just like those of China today. Even today, Japanese banks prop up thousands of "zombie" companies—and the jobs they represent—with cheap credit while Japanese savers effectively earn nothing, even if formal Japanese industrial policy is largely a thing of the past.

The Old Urge to Pick Winners and Losers

The ambition to have political leaders run the economy and pick winners and losers by control of credit and state subsidies is very old. France, before the Revolution and since, has always believed the state should take a leading role in economic management, a policy called *dirigisme* and embraced by French governments of all political shades. Germany after unification in 1871, and before that the Prussian state, demonstrated how enlightened bureaucrats could drive progress. It was the Kingdom of Prussia that first had universal literacy, and imperial Germany invented employment programs and government pensions, and made industrial firms provide decent housing for workers. The Fabian socialists in the United Kingdom and progressives in the United States saw the scenes of squalor and rampant inequality of the late 19th and early 20th centuries, and saw the enlightened activist state embodied in Prussian-led Germany as their model. The record of Germany's rise as an industrial power with minimal social strife was impressive, demonstrating that state power and capitalism in balance was a better way than the free market.

Of course, as usual, things are more complex and nuanced. The rise of Germany (and later, Japan) was a great deal more entrepreneurial than the cartoon version allows. The all-knowing economic-planning bureaucracy in Japan, MITI (Ministry of International Trade and Industry), did not support the creation of a Japanese automobile industry, which was created by a few renegade motor-cycle manufacturers. In the 19th century, no German bureaucrat spotted and targeted investment in the chemical and dyestuff industries, where German research universities provided key breakthroughs. Rather, entrepreneurs built companies around new processes and products that German universities and engineers had perfected first. When examined in detail, as Alfred Chandler of Harvard did in his monumental book *Scale and Scope* (Belknap Press of Harvard University Press, 1994), the strengths of German industry are largely organizational and even cultural. Germans (and Americans of the same period) were capable of organizing and raising capital to build very large, professionally managed firms. So were the Japanese. The British, the inventors of modern industry, failed on both points for the most part for reasons as varied as their financial system, their educational institutions, and notions of social status. In other words, it could be that the Germans and Japanese, along with the American "organization man," were good at big business in an era when being big mattered.

A counterexample is provided by France, where state control of the economy and the importance of exquisitely well-trained bureaucrats has always been taken for granted, as noted previously. France is a place where educational merit lands one in elite institutions like Sciences Po and the other so-called *grandes écoles* designed to train men and women to serve the state, always the font of honor and highest aspiration for the flower of French youth. By doing service to the state, however, these elite cadres also end up doing very well for themselves. The top posts in French banking and industry are to a great extent interchangeable with top posts in the elite government ministries, especially the Treasury and the Bank of France. Although America has some startling examples of people like the Clintons and Al Gore becoming very wealthy through public service, typically it is wealthy men and women who enter politics after making their fortunes (e.g., Michael Bloomberg, Jon Corzine, and Mitt Romney). In France it is a brilliant career as an unelected bureaucrat that leads to the corner office. If rule by the brightest and best was superior to the random and messy processes of what the French disdainfully call Anglo-Saxon capitalism, you would expect France to produce world-class firms. By and large it doesn't, and again it has world leadership in areas staked out by renegade entrepreneurs rather than the "winners" picked by the state. Does anyone equate Thompson-Bull with IBM or Apple?

The Myth of the Laissez-Faire Economy

The opposite myth to the wisdom of elites picking winners and losers is equally shaky when examined. Anglo-Saxon capitalism has never been the free enterprise, laissez-faire paradise lost that many on the political right idealize. From the very beginning, again as noted before, government debt has been the bedrock of our financial markets. Moreover, government direction of credit is old hat and goes back to the early republic, not the New Deal. No sooner had America gained independence than the new state governments were met with a barrage of schemes and proposed measures for the encouragement of industry. The biggest single driver of the industrialization of America in the 19th century was the construction of railways. Much, indeed at times most, of the capital for railroad construction came from Britain (in 1883, US railway shares were 13 percent of the value of all shares and bonds quoted in London), but both federal and state governments provided subsidies and even public land to the railway promoters. The railway companies in turn were able to effectively buy control of state and city governments, especially in the West. In fact, the power of the Southern Pacific Railway in California politics helped spark an era of progressive reform in that state in the 20th century under the legendary governor Hiram Johnson.

What China and other developing markets have in government-directed credit and finance is often denounced as "crony capitalism," an accusation that can also be heard in regard to continental Europe and Japan. Supposedly, US market capitalism is better precisely because neutral and self-interested investors get to pick corporate winners and losers, not the clever and the politically well connected. The great Austrian economist Friedrich Hayek taught that nobody is quite as clever as the market process at allocating capital. There are insuperable limitations to human knowledge and foresight. Price signals, while imperfect, communicate information relevant to investors and entrepreneurs, who essentially make bets on the future. Profits arise when change occurs in the market and someone seizes the opportunity before others. It is all a big experiment, but millions of autonomous decisions by buyers, sellers, and entrepreneurs sort out what works and what doesn't, and the economy advances. Another great Austrian, Joseph Schumpeter, called this process "creative destruction," in which enterprises are constantly dying and being born.

The tidy minds of educated elites have always rebelled at this wasteful process. Surely science and analysis, supported by ever-better models and data, can do better than the random judgment of the financial markets. The progressive mind also suspects, not without justification, that the financial markets and the practice of business are corrupt and rigged by a selfish few. Only a disinterested, democratically legitimate governing elite should make the critical decisions about what to provide money for and what does not deserve investment. Perhaps the most striking post–New Deal example of this has been the notion that government could by force of will create a new "green" economy. Leaving aside the merits of climate science, which I am not qualified to argue, the fact is that modern industrial civilization from its inception has been centered on exploiting fossil fuel. Moreover, technical breakthroughs in oil and gas extraction suggest ample supplies of fossil fuel for longer time horizons than had been imagined even a decade ago—see Daniel Yergin's new book *The Quest* (Penguin, 2011).

Despite this, the current administration took it upon itself to create a new "green" economy by using government loan guarantees, so-called stimulus funds, and above all, regulatory actions adverse to conventional fuels. Major US corporations—never great defenders of the free market—jumped on board the government gravy train, as did well-connected venture capitalists. The bailed-out auto manufacturers, especially General Motors, also had their investment priorities directed to electric cars despite questions about market demand. The Chevy Volt and Solyndra are but two of the poster children of this adventure in central planning, industrial policy, and crony capitalism pursued with the best of intentions.

The Point: Power

Which brings us to the point of why financial repression and industrial policy are two sides of the same coin. The point is power. Power today isn't about owning the means of production in the classic socialist formula, but the ability to direct who gets credit and investment in a public policy framework designed by the great and good. The great and good know who they are, whether products of the *grandes écoles* or Harvard and Princeton. Their frustration with the markets rather than the government picking economic winners and losers based on the irrational preferences of mere consumers is quite understandable. So is their belief that so many successful entrepreneurs and executives lack their education and high mindedness. Markets often make the stupid and the swinish rich. This is obviously terribly unfair to really smart people who have the right academic credentials. I know this, as a holder of multiple Harvard degrees who has managed to escape becoming rich!

Financial repression stealthily confiscates accumulated wealth and adds to governments' ability to "make investments"—that is, spend public money on things (many of them legitimate, such as defense and basic research) that would not be funded by the market. The direction of credit and investment linked to industrial policy (and social policy) is simply how choices get made. Subsidized green energy is but an extreme example, since the Eisenhower national highway system, subsidies for home ownership, and student loans are all examples of using the financial system for essentially nonmarket, noneconomic ends. This kind of thing goes back to the day when royal monopolies were given to joint stock companies to build out the British Empire for broke British monarchs, and it is not going away any time soon. It is all a matter of degree and balance. In the Victorian Era, the markets became free and global for several generations, but that was an anomaly backed by British wealth and sea power along with an almost mystical British belief in free trade. In the 1980s, as Daniel Yergin's now incredibly dated documentary *The Commanding Heights* relates, the financial markets regained some of their freedom after half a century of financial repression and industrial policy. In 2008, the music stopped. The state has regained the commanding heights and is likely to stay there for a very long time.

Taking Risk out of a Risky Business

Since banks and the financial markets more broadly are the only institutions that can blow up the whole economy overnight, there has always been a public interest in limiting the trouble they can cause. There are a number of ways this has been attempted over time.

Keep Them Small

One is to keep banks relatively small, as with England limiting joint-stock banks and the United States allowing state banking laws to limit banks to a single office or jurisdiction. Banks that are private partnerships trade on their owners' funds and are bound to be cautious. Small-town banks were, if not formally, then often practically family businesses. The problem is of course that such banks have limited scale and scope to provide anything but very basic services. In addition, being dependent on few customers and, often, the fortune of one community, they are vulnerable to adverse events. The 1890 Barings crisis in London, triggered by government debt default in Argentina, created such market turmoil that most of the old private partnerships amalgamated into big shareholder-owned banks, the most notable of which was Barclays. Small-town banks in America failed by the thousands in the 1920s and 1930s. While these banks were "small enough to fail," they were often the only banks in town, and their failures caused real distress.

Keep Them Separate

A second approach, which was embodied in the old City of London, was a clear separation of functions between financial market players, many if not most of which were private partnerships, and so-called High Street (in America, we say Main Street) banks that took deposits and ran the payments system. The former included brokers who underwrote shares issues, merchant banks who advised corporate clients, market-makers, and so forth. These were all risking their own money, and all could fail without too much risk to the system. The High Street banks essentially took no risks, lending only on good security, precisely because they were lending customers money.

The Vickers Commission report (September 2011) has recommended that the UK government legislate a form of "ring fencing" that would go back to a version of this High Street/high-finance split, but within one company. The public deposits and payments business would be conducted in a ring-fenced entity with its own, higher capital requirements. The wholesale financial market trading of the company would have to fund itself instead of having use of customer deposits. Whether this can be made to work is a good question, but the principle of not gambling with deposits from the public is appealing.

The United States tried something similar under the Glass-Steagall Act of 1933, which separated investment and commercial banking in a more straightforward way. Under this system, banks can be very big without threatening the deposit money and payments system that Main Street relies on, at least in theory. The objection is that the so-called universal bank model, where commercial and market activities are under one roof, is better for clients (one-stop shopping), but also safer since wholesale financial markets, retail banking, and commercial banking have different cycles and present different risks. A broadly diversified bank is, the argument goes, a safer bank. The Volcker rule, though very hard to implement in practice, is a provision of Dodd-Frank that moves us a way toward restoration of the core principle of Glass-Steagall: that banks should not use customer funds to go to the casino.

Let Them Grow Big

The third way to decrease risk in banking and financing is also by happy coincidence a key lever of financial repression—that is, to allow banks to become large through amalgamation of weak and failing institutions into very large groups, but then impose detailed regulations and rules over every aspect of their activities. These rules are not spelled out in Dodd-Frank, the poster child for this approach, but instead called for, so the 848-page law could spawn scores or hundreds of pages of regulation per page. Glass-Steagall by contrast was all of 37 pages long. As a practical matter, it will be impossible to run a financial institution without being in violation of hundreds of often-contradictory rules and requirements. This will force banks to seek political cover—that is, forgiveness—from the government by doing the bidding of the political class.

One thing Dodd-Frank did not do was solve the too-big-to-fail problems—although large government banks are easier to conduct financial repression and industrial policy through (China being a case in point, as well as France and Japan).

Increase Competition

This brings us to a fourth approach to decreasing risk in the banking system that is not being tried. This is to reduce the megabanks to a reasonable size through positive and negative incentives to shrink their scale and scope, and to increase banking and financial market competition by easing barriers to market entry and exit into and out of banking, and in general leveraging market forces. In theory, the principles of free-market capitalism should also apply to banking. They do not. The problem with general principles is that in practice they can lead to vast mischief. When banks compete in a free market, their incentives are always to take market shares from other banks or to achieve higher profits in their existing business. Both these things tend to push them to take greater risks.

In *Financial Market Meltdown*, I go into some detail about why financial innovation, a product of competition—though often competition to get around regulation—is almost always a dangerous thing because banks end up taking risks that they don't properly understand. As Walter Bagehot sagely advised in *Lombard Street*, a good banker is obliged to turn down any credit that presents an unsecured risk, essentially never lending money to anyone who actually needs it. Competition between banks, and between banks and other forms of finance, such as bonds, would drive all the profits out of risk-free lending very quickly.

In *Financial Market Meltdown*, I argued that "the mix of politics and finance is always going to be toxic and dangerous to the taxpayer." I neglected to add that competition and finance is always going be dangerous to the economy. The old rule is that you can have a competitive financial system, as we did between the 1980s and 2008, or a safe system, as we had during the 50 years of financial repression, but you can't have both. Competition between banks was muted by sheer size and collusion in the United Kingdom and Canada, by regulation in the United States, and by a government-managed convoy system in Japan that effectively prevented banks from competing with each other before financial liberalization set in 30 years ago. The record of bank failures and financial crises since market liberalization is sobering. Moreover, crises tend to stem from plain, dumb lending and herd behavior rather than casino-like behavior in the wholesale financial markets. In fact, the most dangerous things banks can do might just be lending money to consumers for house purchases.

Death Knell for Consumer Credit

The American economy has been to a remarkable extent driven by consumption, with the Personal Consumption Expenditure (PCE) share of GDP at 70 percent, about 10 points above the average for the industrial world. Some of this is cultural. American optimism about future prospects and lack of shame about owing money are surely factors. However, much of the consumption-driven prosperity of America stems from financial innovations, ranging from the widespread introduction of charge accounts by merchants a century ago to the widespread securitization of consumer credit from mortgages to car loans in the decades leading up to the crisis. Although Paul Volcker famously said that the only positive financial innovation he could think of was the ATM, and I take a swipe at financial innovation, as noted previously, there is a very important and positive type of financial innovation that we need to carefully nurture. I am talking about the application of modern technologies, especially telecommunications and computing, that vastly increase the effectiveness of sound banking practice. Walter Bagehot in *Lombard Street* saw the advantage of the new and controversial joint-stock banks in something like mass production because "the ways of lending money safely are few in number, easily learned and admit of no variation." This meant that banks expand beyond the limits of personal relationships between lender and borrower and instead build "loan factories," and for that matter "payments factories," based on armies of clerks and piles of paper reaching up to the sky. The application of information technology to these processes reduces people and paper, making it immensely cheaper to run a bank on a per-account or per-transaction basis. This allows a much larger portion of the population to be banked—that is, to have a transaction account and often access to revolving credit.

It is hard to find any downside in automation of clerical routine to reduce costs, but the upside has been arguably much greater. Information logistics has become so efficient that vast quantities of information can be exchanged and analyzed to make transactions between borrowers and savers, and buyers and sellers, more secure and less liable to counterparty default or other downsides. The same exponential increase in data richness and advanced modeling techniques—sometimes called "big data"—make possible far more targeted and efficient marketing and sales, risk management, and product development in retail finance and a host of other service businesses.

Cutting Off the Consumer

The threat to such progress posed by financial repression needs thoughtful assessment. If bank balance sheets are skewed toward funding the state and its rent-seekers, as seems to be happening throughout the post-crisis landscape, we could find ourselves back in the world before 1980 when finance companies and retailers (and loan sharks), not the commercial banks, provided most consumer credit aside from mortgages (which were the province of savings banks). The banks took over this business of consumer lending by making vast investments in building out efficient electronic systems to source, evaluate, analyze, score, price, and service credit as a mass-market product, not just the preserve of the affluent few. As noted in Chapter 3, excessive and ill-considered reregulation could end up inadvertently "unbanking the banked." In a general atmosphere of financial repression, consumers are likely to find themselves at the back of the line for bank credit for many years, indeed decades. In an economy that is so consumer driven, eliminating or degrading the financial industry's incentives for making the capital required for extending the revolution in information technology into retail finance is shortsighted. Unduly restricting the availability of credit needed by households to bridge the peaks and valleys of the income and expenditure is a huge risk to prosperity and economic growth.

Starving the Entrepreneurs

Financial repression is also associated with a world where entrepreneurs and start-ups find it almost impossible to get the funds they need to survive and prosper. Japan, Germany, and France, all poster children for financial repression, make life extremely difficult for any enterprise or entrepreneur without political and social connections. The United States used to be the great exception to all this. No longer will this salient advantage exist if things are allowed to go too far down the current path.

Of course, people are inventive, and the development of financial innovations of a less wholesome sort—especially the so-called shadow banking system and the growth of loosely regulated offshore financial centers—was the direct result of the last great era of financial repression. Exotic capital-market instruments that nobody understands are not the product of a sound regulatory regime. They are the toxic fruit of a stifling regulatory hothouse.

The massive and almost impossible-to-comprehend reregulation of the global financial system is just beginning. There is still time to stop the worst excesses, but politicians are unlikely to do so given the universal bad name of banks and bankers. Not that bank lobbyists have been idle. The top bankers have managed to preserve the two worst features of the pre-crisis system: a perverse incentive system for top management and traders that turn accounting profits into cash for senior employees, and the concentration of banking assets (and risk) into a few too-big-to-fail institutions that governments are obliged to prop up.

We will return to those subjects in Chapter 7. Suffice it here to say that the new megabanks that arise from the ongoing crisis will be even more difficult to properly comprehend and manage than the largest financial conglomerates before 2008. Micro-regulation of the activities of banks that are not subject to market discipline is unlikely to succeed in preventing the next crisis, which will be inevitable and most likely as unexpected as all of its predecessors over the centuries. Financial regulators cannot be shown to have predicted or prevented a financial panic in all of history. Only an arrogant and naïve view of what clever men and women drafting laws can accomplish would suggest otherwise.

The next chapter will review the global economic interconnections and forces that might bring us to an even more severe crisis before we have finished nailing shut the barn door on finance.

Global Whirlwinds

Why We Are All in This Together

In the previous chapter, I noted that it was both natural and mistaken to look upon the finances of a country as if it were a household. It is equally misleading to think that a country's finances can be viewed in isolation from those of all other countries it trades with and in which it invests money or raises capital. Yet that is precisely what the political class and the general public naturally do.

Global Trade Is Not a Zero-Sum Game

The basic math is simple. If one country sells more stuff to another country than it buys in return, a trade deficit arises in the first country and a trade surplus in the second. These add up to zero, being mirror images of each other, and it is natural to assume that this is a zero-sum game where surplus countries win and deficit countries lose. However, bilateral trade is actually almost never in balance because countries have different stages of economic development and different business cycles, as well as different advantages in producing specific goods, services, and commodities.

This is even more true when looking at multilateral trade, since every country actually trades and invests with many other countries at once. It is quite common for a country to enjoy a large bilateral trade surplus with one country and bilateral deficits with several others. The balancing mechanism is investment. The classic case in the contemporary world is China and the United States, which is red meat for political demagoguery in this election year. Fundamentally, China enjoys low manufacturing costs (though this advantage is diminishing as wages rise), and both European and American multinational corporations conduct some portion of their assembly operations in China, often through many layers of subcontractors. The assembled goods—such as your basic 72-inch flat-screen TV—have to be sold abroad because the same wages that make them cheap to make in China make it hard to sell many of them there (though this too is gradually changing). The result is that Best Buy and Wal-Mart can sell the flat-screen TVs at prices far below what they would otherwise cost, so many more Americans can buy them than would otherwise be the case. If you like big-screen TVs, that is no bad thing. China in return gets nothing but scraps of paper (actually the electronic equivalent) called dollars. Remember, these are not like the silver dollars of the 19th century that could actually be spent in China; they are purely promises to pay that are only usable in the US financial system. All the Chinese exporter can do as a practical matter is turn them into local currency at the official rate. In other words, the exporter must sell the dollars to the Chinese Central Bank. The Chinese Central Bank ends up with a vast pile of claims on the United States—$3.2 trillion dollars as of this writing—and other Western financial systems. Its only recourse is to invest most of it in US financial assets. The highest-quality and lowest-risk US financial assets are of course the debt of the federal government or agencies with some form of government guarantee.

Cheap TVs Will Continue to Be a Good Deal for the United States

The very fact that so much money needs to be parked in the US Treasury market helps keep rates low, indeed negative in real terms. In other words, the value of China's reserves will tend to shrink by the logic of financial repression—China is simply the largest captive investor. Those 72-inch TVs seem a better swap all the time. The key issue for China is how to maintain the value of these reserves in local currency terms so they can actually be used in China at some point. The answer is to try to maintain a fixed relationship between the Chinese RMB and the dollar through central bank regulations and market operations in China. Otherwise, the money China earned making and selling the TVs would simply melt away as the dollar lost value and the RMB gained value in the currency markets. This is always the case, because when a country runs a trade surplus, its currency becomes stronger relative to the promises to pay being pumped out the deficit country in exchange for goods. Absent the Chinese authorities' actions to keep the RMB from appreciating too much relative to the dollar, Chinese internal costs would be much higher.

Currency Manipulation or Fair Dealing?

This is why China regularly stands accused of *currency manipulation*—an unfair trade policy in the eyes of American politicians. The "problem" of the Chinese trade surplus with the United States is simplistically attributed to artificially low Chinese costs in dollar terms. The truth cuts both ways: if China did not carefully restrict the use of its currency in international markets—in banker-speak, if the RMB was freely convertible at market prices—its currency would no doubt be substantially higher in dollar terms. That would aid other developing markets that depend on low-cost labor to compete internationally, and it would raise the cost of Chinese goods to United States consumers considerably, so Americans would learn to do without their 72-inch TVs in many instances. That does not mean that the "jobs" supposedly "shipped" to China would return to high-cost, high-tax, and high-regulation localities in the United States. The development of global supply chains, "lean manufacturing," and offshore production are responses to increased global competition and technologies that change factor costs while shrinking time and distance. Even doubling the value of the RMB in dollar terms would change none of that.

On the other hand, removing Chinese savings and reserves from the global financial economy could be catastrophic. The same politicians who bang on about getting tough with China routinely vote for spending that depends on Chinese purchases of US Treasury debt. The super-low interest rates of the Great Moderation sowed the seeds of the asset-price bubbles that led up to the financial market meltdown of 2008 were in part a reflection of too much Chinese money chasing dollar investments. However, going forward, the lack of Chinese investment flows could prove far more dangerous in the current state of the world.

If your memories go back to the 1980s, you'll remember that the trade deficit with Japan and its currency policies attracted the same mixture of panic and vitriol that China inspires today. Unlike China, Japan depended on the United States for national security and always had to bow to US pressures to let the yen appreciate against the dollar. Japanese trade surpluses vis-à-vis the United

States persisted as Japan's domestic economy imploded after 1989, creating a long off-and-on recession, curbing domestic income growth and demand, something a rapidly aging Japanese population also contributed to. The healthy part of the Japanese economy continues to be export industry, though much production has moved to China and other low-cost countries. Japan continues to be the biggest foreign holder of US dollar debt outside of China—indeed, the biggest creditor in the world. In other words, the China story is scarcely new; it is largely a replay of Japan on a larger scale, with foreign multinationals instead of Japanese corporations leading the charge.

Ants and Grasshoppers

Basically, China and Japan (and we could add Germany to form the trifecta of export powerhouses) represent high-savings, frugal cultures with highly productive manufacturing sectors. (China was once just cheap, but now it is getting really good at making things and intends to become a high-value player.) Frugal exporters can only exist in a world where people in other countries are big spenders and save little, but the frugal exporters feel virtuous. (It is possible to be frugal without being an exporter, of course, but such countries are almost always poor.) They are the thrifty, hardworking ants and paragons of virtue. However, the decadent and lazy grasshoppers resent them, as they find virtue creepy and dislike those to whom they owe money.

The ants and grasshoppers are, in fact, dependent on each other. The formal term *global imbalance*—a topic that sage economic commentator Martin Wolf often returns to in the pages of the *Financial Times* as a core threat to global prosperity—is largely one of too much saving in Asia, and too much spending in Europe and especially the United States. The ideal solution—one China has specifically targeted in its 12th five-year plan (yes, China is still formally a communist country with five-year plans)—is for much higher domestic consumption in the countries that save too much, and higher savings in countries that scarcely save at all, such as the United States and United Kingdom. China is addressing its tax code to boost disposable income and beginning to build out a basic social safety net to reduce the incentives for its citizens to save. There are signs of progress already toward achieving a more balanced growth model that is less dependent on exports and government spending on infrastructure. Such transitions are tricky to execute, however, and a China that exports less (and this is happening due to weakness in Europe and the United States) earns less to lend its Western customers to buy its stuff—a downward demand spiral that can end badly.

Why China and the United States Are Joined at the Hip

Niall Ferguson has popularized the term *Chimerica* to describe two very different countries joined at the hip in one cross-Pacific economy. Although they sell a bit more to Europe, the Chinese sell more to the United States than any other single country and in turn provide America with much cheaper goods than it could produce at home. China also provides the money to allow bank credit to flow to the buyers of those goods and government debt funding for programs to support US incomes and demand. China makes and saves; America buys and borrows. Ferguson sees the arrangement coming to an end, which cannot be good for America. Since the 2008 financial market meltdown, China has, after an initial body blow to its exports, managed to massively stimulate its economy with vast infusions of bank credit and public spending. This has made it the engine of the global economy—the "last man standing," as Duff McDonald described Jamie Dimon's leadership of J. P. Morgan in the wake of the crisis.

Now the global last man standing is showing signs of fatigue. The massive spending and low rates have lit inflationary fires, which feed through into labor demands for higher pay and worry stability-obsessed authorities. There are signs of a real estate bubble fueled by cheap money and overbuilding. Headline growth rates have fallen. While the chronically ignorant in America fear the inexorable rise of China and envy its planned economy, most well-informed market participants wonder if an overheated and bubble-prone China can achieve a soft landing with slower, less-inflationary growth. The alternative is really unpleasant to contemplate.

China is not only a big exporter to the United States and European Union, but the largest customer of both in many sectors. With the rich developed world limping along with little or no growth, China is becoming not just the lender of last resort, but the buyer of last resort for the whole global economy. Countries that have fared relatively well since 2008, including Brazil, Canada, Australia, and Germany, sell raw materials and producer goods such as machine tools to China. These countries in turn can buy stuff from the United States and each other because Chinese demand gives them trade surpluses to spend. Knock Chinese growth down several notches, and this all comes unstuck, leaving the global economy sidelined without a locomotive—a role the United States can no longer to play. And it could get much worse.

China is a vast country of 1.3 billion people, which has always been difficult to hold together except in circumstances of relative stability and social harmony imposed by the state. The current Chinese state is the product of a revolution and series of repressions that were shocking even by 20th century standards in terms of lives lost. The legitimacy of the Communist Party and its ability to govern with a gloved fist rests on two pillars: regaining China's independence and dignity after generations of foreign interference and aggression on one hand, and giving its people far higher living standards than they have ever experienced on the other. The first pillar is emotional; the second is cold reality: accept Communist rule without demur and get a chance to be rich and comfortable. Take away the rich-and-comfortable bit, which is based on unprecedented 10-plus percent year-on-year growth for decades, and all bets are off. The Chinese are acutely conscious of their history and know that on many occasions it has suffered sudden collapses into chaos. Rather than worry about China stealing American jobs, Americans should wish them well in rebalancing their economy toward sustainable development.

It often seems that the biggest threat to China's continued success (and by extension that of the global economy) is a trade war. The United States has a bad history of starting trade wars, given the low level of public discourse and the power of special interests in Congress. The notorious Smoot-Hawley Tariff of 1930 helped pave the way for Hitler and Tojo to gain power, and thus bears some responsibility for the real-world war that soon followed. The generation that experienced the Second World War created institutions to help prevent a recurrence of the 1930s, so there is some hope that overt trade wars can be prevented, at least for a while. The less overt threat to the global system is austerity.

Why Austerity Can Be Worse Than Debt

Austerity is a word that sounds like the embodiment of virtue. In reality, it is very unpleasant, like coming down off hard drugs. To count as real austerity, government spending has to be cut in real terms—not the phony cuts we hear about in US politics, where a slight reduction in the rate of spending increase poses as a "cut," or, even better, a "mean-spirited" and "painful" cut. Austerity means that people who are used to getting money from the government get less of it, while people whose money is taken in taxes to be given away don't see their taxes go down. Austerity is living within one's means applied to the state. It has always induced a big economic contraction, as with the "lost decade" of the 1980s in Latin America, when the IMF forced countries that had over-borrowed and overspent to impose austerity as a condition of getting loans. This approach to economic reform worked, but at the cost of wiping out huge swaths of the middle class in countries such as Mexico, though with the upside of discrediting a one-party crony-capitalist system. As I argued in the last chapter, countries that have effective control of their own currencies and, critically, can borrow from captive domestic savers, will always prefer to administer a dose of financial repression and inflation instead of the bitter (and politically suicidal in many cases) medicine of austerity.

The Euro: Meant to Pave the Way to Real Unification

This brings us to the heart of the matter concerning the European debt crisis. The single currency, the euro, was supposed to drive something called economic convergence in a single market for goods and services. This was supposed to smooth the way for a "deepening" of the European Union until the sovereign powers of the individual states would be largely subsumed into European institutions. A more cynical reading is that the political calculation among those in favor of full European integration was that if the experiment of a single currency failed, the resulting crisis would panic the voters of Europe, whose consent for the enterprise was never obtained, into accepting it.

This helps to explain why every time the two top countries in Europe get on the same page about the ongoing debt debacle, they (sometimes referred to as *Merkozey*—a blending of the names of Nicolas Sarkozy, France's President until May of 2012, and German Chancellor Angela Merkel) talk about treaties and "more Europe, not less." The crisis is being addressed largely on the level of high politics—saving and expanding the "European Project"—rather than practical economic reality. And for good reason: there is no good answer to the problems the euro has created for the European economy from its inception.

The European Project created a European Central Bank (ECB) with considerable political independence and a very high degree of professionalism to give credibility to the new currency. It did not give that bank powers to lend directly to governments, for the same reason that all other major central banks are so constrained, which is that politicians would turn them into piggy banks and inflate away the value of the money issued by the central bank. So-called central bank credibility is all that makes fiat money worth more than a tinker's damn. Once it is lost, it is almost impossible to regain. Other than prop up the banking systems themselves, there is a limit to what the ECB can do. The rest is politics.

Living Like Germany

The politics are simple enough. The euro allowed every country that joined it to borrow as if they were Germany, the largest and most fiscally prudent (except for the very costly process of its national reunification in the 1990s) country in Europe. This view of sovereign euro debt was really a judgment of the markets that no EU member would be allowed to default. In the United States, by contrast, every state and local government has a credit rating that reflects its spending and borrowing habits to at least some degree, and many have far higher borrowing costs than the federal government, although it is hard to imagine Washington letting prodigal states as large as California or Illinois actually default. If Greece and Portugal had to borrow on this basis, they would not have been tempted to use the miracle of low-interest-rate borrowing to boost public spending. But they did just that, despite having signed on to the fiscal rules designed to prevent runaway deficit spending. The rules were honored in the breach anyway—Germany was the first to exceed the deficit limits agreed to by treaty. The politics of more and more Europeans living like Germans, because their governments could borrow like Germany and spend lavishly, were too good to mess around with, so nobody did.

The global market meltdown of 2008 brought the party to a halt, but not at once. At first, Europe saw the American banking system crisis as a vindication for its social-economy model over rapacious Anglo-Saxon capitalism. Then it became evident that some of the peripheral countries of Europe, notably Greece, could not service, let alone roll over, their debt. This is where the free ride for all turned into a political standoff that has yet to be resolved. The Germans hold all the cards, at least superficially. Unlike other countries, it has enormous credibility in the financial markets (when Standard & Poor's downgraded debt of 17 countries on Friday the 13th, 2012, Germany retained its Triple A rating), and its export-led economy has been growing better than most industrial countries. The problem is that the Germans will not fund Greece and other Mediterranean countries' lifestyles unless they become virtuous and frugal like themselves. Germans demand real austerity from "Club Med," lest it end up supporting the hopelessly spendthrift south with its hard work and high taxes.

The problem with this is that economic demand in these countries is heavily dependent on government spending programs and payrolls. Slash these and you plunge these countries into depression and even risk revolutionary movements springing up on the left and right, something nobody wants to risk given the history of the 1930s. In fact, the history of Europe in the 1940s makes the Germans easy political targets in Greece and elsewhere if they push their demands for austerity and economic reforms too far.

One of the ironies of the whole drama is that although many Germans would like to return to their beloved Deutsche Mark and leave the euro to the profligate, the German business community knows better. The German exporters sell on quality and innovation, but there is a point at which an expensive currency just prices you out of whole markets. The euro makes German goods more affordable to other Europeans than if they had retained their previous, weaker national currencies. Equally, although the euro has been expensive in dollar terms for several years, overall it has probably been cheaper than the old Deutsche Mark would have been given the same German export success. In this sense, it has had some of the same benefits as the currency manipulation that China (and before that Japan) has been pilloried for over the years. Nobody can be certain of the costs for any country of leaving the euro—or, if a major country defaults, the costs staying in. The Maastricht Treaty—the treaty that launched the European Union—left no line of retreat; joining the euro was specifically intended to be an irreversible decision with no escape hatches allowed. That said, major banks and corporations around the world are beginning to think the unthinkable and plan for the collapse of the euro under different scenarios.

Why a European Banking Crisis Threatens America

The 1990s saw the substantial concentration of deposits in the largest institutions within the US banking system, and the 2008 panic triggered shotgun weddings that put a capstone on the progress. Today, the majority of the US banking and payments system operates within and between seven or eight banks. These same banks provide much of the short-term funding and liquidity needed by an even more concentrated investment-banking industry, as well as the clearing and settlement of trades on the stock exchanges. They also act as prime brokers to the giant hedge fund industry. This is precisely why the Federal Reserve had no choice but to keep these institutions afloat after Lehman collapsed. Whatever the current law might say, the Fed again would again have no other choice if another shock hit the system in the future. As a practical matter, the global financial system is so thoroughly integrated that the same applies to giant European- and Asian-headquartered banks operating in New York and London that form part of the same highly concentrated system of short- and medium-term credit between financial institutions.

Under normal circumstances, the whole global banking and finance system operates like one big happy family in which everyone trusts one another. Banks can lend money in excess of their deposits not only because they can issue medium- and long-term debt in the market, but because they can borrow funds overnight from one another in the interbank market. European banks can lend their clients dollars because they can issue short-term paper to US money market funds. They can also hedge their interest rate and currency risks with each other and to customers by doing swaps and trading other derivatives with each other. These activities are all absolutely routine and essential to making the system work. They are also global, with the same big banks operating in multiple centers, including New York, London, Tokyo, and Singapore.

The little-appreciated fact is that the world has a very diverse national banking system that interacts in a single global money market. This means that many banks borrow foreign currency, especially dollars, to make loans or take trading positions. The "spreads" on these borrowings are normally small, since only highly rated banks are in the market and Basel capital requirements for loans between highly rated banks are modest. Every banking system needs an interbank money market, because at any point in time, some banks will have more deposits than they need and some less. In the United States, this is the so-called *federal funds market*, but banks also raise funds with commercial paper (essentially marketable IOUs) and *repos*, short for "repurchase agreements" (overnight loans against collateral, normally government bonds), as well as in the bond market. For the large global banks based outside the United States, and therefore without domestic dollar deposits, the ability to tap these sources is normally taken for granted, as it is for the big US institutions whose lending and trading businesses vastly exceed their own deposits.

It's Still All About Trust

The canary in the mineshaft leading up to the 2008 financial market meltdown was that banks in the interbank-lending market began to get very nervous about the creditworthiness of one another and ramped up prices (the key one being the London Interbank Offered Rate [LIBOR]) while cutting back supply. The market froze up and has never become completely unfrozen since; it's down 60 percent from its pre-crisis peak as I write. The original deterioration of mutual trust in the market was based on worries about which banks had big, illiquid positions in dud securities backed by US mortgages. Today, the culprit is called *sovereign risk*—the fear that some banks are sitting on government bonds that might become worthless or take a big haircut in the event of a default by Greece or other weak links in the euro system. The total collapse of the interbank-lending market is no longer viewed as an unthinkable event, as evidenced by dramatic recent actions by the ECB.

Some of the big sources of short-term dollar funding for the European banks have gone on strike, notably the huge US-based money market funds that at one time were attracted by the yield on European bank dollar commercial paper. The ECB has stepped into the breach, lending vast sums of dollars to European banks that, collectively, have some $700 billion in loans coming due in 2012—loans the private markets probably would not roll over. Of course, the ECB has no ability to create dollars to lend, but it gets them from the Federal Reserve through swap lines between the two. The latest emergency measure, taken in December of 2011, is for the ECB to lend to banks at 1 percent for three years. It gave €489 billion to 523 banks on December 21 alone. An article in *the Economist* newspaper reported at the time, "The European Central Bank has come under criticism for its failure to act as lender of last resort to embattled sovereigns. Yet when it comes to banks, the traditional recipients of central bank support, the ECB is lender of last resort on steroids" ("The ECB, eternal and infinite," December 21, 2011).

Steroids or not, the point of the operation is to prevent, or rather slow, the silent run on Europe's banks that has already begun. There is ample evidence that deposits are leaving banks in the shakier countries, such as Greece and Italy. Giving comfort to the markets that the banks won't become insolvent over the next three years makes sense. But when you step back, the picture is very disconcerting. Basically, Europe's weaker economies might have to default or leave the euro, or at least force investors to take big losses on their sovereign lending exposures. Once the first domino goes over, likely Greece, the markets might push much larger countries such as Italy and Spain into the tank. Europe's banks are stuffed with this sovereign paper, some of it the result of open-ended borrowing to save the banks. This, for example, occurred in Ireland, which had sound government finances before the 2008 crisis hit its banks. The banks are now propping up the governments, and unlike the governments they can at least borrow at 1 percent from the ECB (many government bond auctions in Europe have produced ruinous interest rates of 7 or 8 percent or worse). Banks dependent on the ECB cannot borrow elsewhere, so until the market sees an end to the crisis, the ECB program is essentially just buying time. The ECB in turn needs open-ended but discrete backup lines from the Federal Reserve. Meanwhile, curtailed bank lending and government austerity is pushing Europe into recession; 2012 will be an interesting year.

All of this would be somewhat academic, like observing a train wreck from a distance, if the European banks did not have thousands of outstanding financial contracts, from loans to foreign exchange deals to derivatives, payable to the biggest American banks. Recession in Europe will also drive down the sales of American goods and services to Europe, and by extension damage the ability of US firms to borrow, service existing debt, and hire workers, further damping the earnings prospects of American banks.

The Global Money Pump

In the previous section, I neglected to provide a sense of how large the global interbank money market really was. The sums of money—which is to say promises to pay—passed from institution to institution are incomprehensible. It was news in January of 2012 that the US national debt had exceeded GDP at over $15 trillion. A trillion is a very hard number to get one's mind around. However, the gross value exchanged in the leading global clearing and settlement systems in 2010 was $608 trillion in the US Federal Reserve's Fedwire system, $365 trillion in the New York Clearing House CHIPS system, $835 trillion in the ECB TARGET system, and $291 trillion in the Bank of Japan's BOJ.NET system—a total of $2,099 trillion, or 140 times US GDP. There were hundreds of trillions more paid between banks in other central bank systems around the world, and hundreds of trillions more in transactions that are netted between parties either bilaterally or in clearinghouses for securities, commodities, and derivatives. The world economy has around $70 trillion in total output per year in goods and services, a sum that the interbank and securities markets flip over several times a week in trading activity.

Many commentators, including Lord Turner of the UK Financial Services Authority, have questioned the social utility of all this financial market trading. Leading continental European countries have embraced the idea of a so-called Tobin tax, essentially a small percentage of each ticket, on wholesale financial trades to reduce incentives to trade and raise revenue for EU states, a move bitterly opposed by the UK, which forms the epicenter of all this activity. Certainly, interbank trading seems only loosely connected to the real economy, and as long as governments backstop the big banks, it looks a lot like a game in which the punters can win big but will always get their debts paid off if they lose. This however, misses an important function that the financial system performs in a market economy: *price discovery*. Essentially, prices are only real when buyers and sellers in real life transactions agree on them.

Writing on January 10, 2012 in the *Financial Times* series "Capitalism in Crisis," John Gapper noted the seemingly shocking fact that foreign exchange trading volumes had increased 234 fold (23,000 percent) between 1977 and 2010. At first blush this is a shocking number, but only if you have no context (a common state for financial journalists). The key point is that before the 1930s there existed a global gold standard that kept foreign exchange rates anchored in very tight ranges. After 1945, the Bretton Woods system held exchange rates in tight ranges against the dollar with a looser link to gold, but after the US abandoned the system, rates floated with no anchor to anything. The price of a currency was a market price set by foreign exchange traders in relation to other currencies, at least among so-called convertible currencies. Many countries retained more or less strict controls on purchases and sales of their domestic currencies, but the currencies of large free-market economies were priced by supply and demand in the market, and this remains the case.

Large banks operating in London and other financial centers soon found it profitable to make markets in currencies for forward delivery, taking positions that they might want to hedge. The end users of foreign currency, often international corporations with foreign customers and suppliers, found it useful to hedge their exposures to movements in the currencies they were going to receive or have to pay in the future. Soon, commodity exchanges began selling contracts, just like pork-belly futures, on the future value of various currencies. They did the same with interest rates. Banks and their customers were able to lock in future currency values and interest rates through swaps. At first these were worked out case by case, but they became standard exchange-traded derivatives over time.

The vast majority—perhaps 80 percent—of the gross settlements just mentioned in fact relate to foreign exchange and simple financial futures. This was not just casino gambling, which might indeed apply to some markets, such as equity trading, but a vast improvement in price discovery, the market price of a currency being set around the world in fractions of a second. Does too much "professional" bank-to-bank trading go on relative to the actual needs of end users of foreign currency? Perhaps, but things that have no economic utility rarely thrive, a point many critics of finance tend to ignore.

Technology vs. Friction

What makes this subject so prone to serious misunderstanding is that there has been a revolution in technology that few nonspecialists understand. Before the Bretton Woods agreement broke down in 1971, most foreign exchange trading was conducted in local markets, especially London, by telephone. Other transactions were conducted by "cable," still the nickname of dollar-sterling trading, and clearing and settling was done using correspondent banks. For example, a banker in London would need German marks, but the market for marks against sterling would be thin compared to the dollar market for both currencies. So he would use sterling to buy dollars and use the dollars to buy marks. To settle this trade, he would send a telex to his New York bank, instructing him to pay Clearinghouse funds to another New York bank, which held the dollar account of the German bank that sold him the marks. The actual payment would literally be a paper check cleared through the New York Clearing House, which the bank would be able to use after 10 a.m. the next day.

This was obviously an extremely clumsy procedure, and a risky one. Since instructions were manually processed, the whole procedure was prone to errors. Also, the New York Clearing House could unwind its settlement if a member could not cover the net sum due. Only when the settlement totals were paid in Federal Reserve money was a payment final and irrevocable. However, everyone had cheerfully lived with this way of settling foreign exchange trades for generations up to 1971. There just wasn't that much business under the stable rates of Bretton Woods or the gold standard before. Then, overnight, the global foreign exchange market grew by leaps and bounds as currencies were allowed to float against each other in market trading.

This is where the revolution in technology comes into play. If there is a great deal of friction in making a market transaction, as Nobel Prize–winning economist Ronald Coase pointed out 80 years ago, it will tend to be replaced by bureaucratic command and control or not occur at all. This is why so much "business" takes place within huge corporations instead of free markets. Bretton Woods was very much a bureaucratic solution worked out between governments. Ending it opened up a huge scope for market transactions overnight, but the friction encountered was monumental. The key steps in a market transaction are finding a counterparty to take the other side of the trade; qualifying the counterparty as trustworthy; price discovery, which is essentially using the market to determine if the counterparty is offering or taking a fair price; executing the trade—essentially making a contract; and settling the trade (i.e., paying or getting paid).

When you think about it, you probably do a lot of this through the Web when shopping online. And that is the whole point: information technology makes things possible that otherwise would simply not happen, both in everyday life and in finance. Starting with the foreign exchange market in the 1970s, information technology began to take the friction and costs out of each of the steps while vastly improving quality and richness of transaction data. The telephone markets morphed into screen-based trading systems, streaming market data enabled up-to-the-second price discovery, risk systems dynamically allocated credit lines, and execution moved online. However, the biggest friction breakthrough was probably the least understood but costliest part of the entire value chain described previously: clearing and settlement.

The Clearing and Settlement Bottleneck

The New York Clearing House was initially swamped by the explosion in foreign exchange trade settlements in 1971, but luckily had already been working on a Clearing House Interbank Payment System (CHIPS), which went live in 1972. CHIPS replaced paper checks with computer entry of the payment instructions that New York banks received from their correspondents. These instructions were still a mass of unformatted telexes, cables, and faxes from around the world. Up to one message in five caused an error in

CHIPS, resulting in an explosion in the number of research and adjustment clerks needed in bank back offices. The industry eventually came up with a global standards organization called SWIFT (Society for Worldwide Interbank Financial Telecommunications), which turned bank instructions into standard messages over a dedicated network.

The system went live in 1978, a year after the base year for the shocking 23,000 percent increase in trading quoted previously. The ramp up in volume of trades never would have happened without SWIFT, which eventually led to a *straight-through* procession of trades, meaning that all the necessary bank-to-bank messages to complete the trade go from computers in one bank to computers in another without human intervention—and therefore without errors. The net result is that a trade that cost $15 or 20 dollars to settle in 1972 costs pennies today. Front-end trading systems take out other friction costs. The net result is that the price difference for which a trade makes economic sense for the participants has become far smaller. It is now routine to move hundreds of millions of notional dollars to make a few thousand.

The tidy official mind might balk at this, but prices of currencies (and other financial assets where technology has had the same effect) are now set with far more precision 24/7 globally than would otherwise be the case. If the world is to live with a system of pure "fiat money" (whether the world should is another matter), is this market efficiency and transparency actually a problem? It should also be noted that the tidy official mind has taken a great deal of the risk out of the global settlement system.

In 1974, when CHIPS and the foreign exchange markets were just ramping up, there was an incident where a small private bank in Germany, Bank Herstatt, failed and was shut at the end of the business day in Frankfurt by the German authorities. That was 11:00 a.m. in New York, so the CHIPS system was just beginning to process foreign exchange settlements from European correspondents of the New York banks. The system ground to a halt when news of the German bank's failure became known. In a clearinghouse, the ability of one bank to make good on its obligations is entirely dependent on other banks paying it what they owe. Herstatt could no longer pay what it owed various banks in Germany—so would those banks pay on its instructions in New York? If not, who would be short and how much? How many payments would be impacted by the shortfall? The problem was only resolved when the Federal Reserve got the clearinghouse banks to exchange information and resume making payments to each other in CHIPS. Everyone involved had been terrified, because the incident laid bare how the failure of banks in one time zone could leave big exposures in another in the new regime of active foreign currency trading between banks worldwide.

The War Against Settlement Risk

The story of central bank intervention in shoring up the plumbing of the interbank settlement system starts with the discovery of Herstatt risk and is ongoing. The result was that the Bank for International Settlements (BIS), the club of leading central banks, in Basel formed a standing Committee of Payment and Settlement Systems (the CPSS) that in time devised a global standard for interbank payment systems, called Real Time Gross Settlement (RTGS). RTGS has mostly replaced the ancient clearinghouse practice of netting payments to achieve the smallest possible cash settlement. To do RTGS, a system needs to make each individual payment final and irrevocable, something that requires the use of central bank money and some way of using a combination of timing, periodic netting, and collateralized credit to keep the payments to and from participants flowing. This is a very expensive undertaking, but almost every country with a developed financial system now has an RTGS system based on BIS principles. Parallel efforts by the CPSS have also addressed risk in securities settlements.

The net effect of these measures may have been to prevent a terrible repetition of the single recorded Herstatt crisis, but in fact we will never know. What it clearly did was shift a great deal of settlement risk from private clearinghouses (and therefore their bank owners) to central banks. This took settlement risk out of the enormous increase in trading volume and value. The central banks also eventually came to support a private-sector initiative that led to the establishment of the Continuous Linked Settlement (CLS) Bank in London, which allows major foreign exchange–dealing banks to net their trades with each other before RTGS settlement. Since the top ten foreign exchange–trading banks (all CLS members) account for most of one another's business, CLS greatly reduces the volumes in the RTGS systems, which would be materially higher without it.

The resulting risk-reduction regime has proven robust in the recent crisis, but mainly because the central banks were liberal in providing banks the cash to pay their counterparties. Whether the whole edifice of the RTGS systems was worth the many billions of dollars the industry needed to pour into adapting to them cannot be proven one way or another. What is clear is that only a handful of very large global banks have been able to afford the massive investments in technology required to be "global transaction banks" for the rest of the financial industry and for multinational corporations. Of these, only one is a US institution, and the rest are European (even though their largest volumes are in New York). Also note that SWIFT and the CLS Bank are both based in Europe. Whether Americans like those facts or even understand them, the plumbing of the financial system is truly global, and the fate of our banking system and that of Europe are joined at the hip.

When the news channels treat the fact that the Federal Reserve provided foreign banks operating in the US many hundreds of billions of dollars at the height of the crisis as a scandal, they neglect to explain that without those funds these banks could have failed, bringing our markets to a standstill. We really are all in this together.

Why Finance Might Move to Asia

It is commonplace that capital goes where it is well treated. If that were really true, however, the continued strength and creativity of the financial industry in New York would be a mystery. If fact, finance is largely a people business, and financial centers over time build up a patina of good living for the financial elite —think London theatre and New York restaurants—that make market participants reluctant to pull up stakes. However, in 1961 there was a wholesale invasion of London by US banks fleeing the ill-considered Interest Equalization Tax, with far ranging consequences discussed in *Financial Market Meltdown*. Although London was never more than an outpost, its essentially unregulated markets let the big US banks reinvent themselves while they in turn transformed "the City" beyond recognition.

Given the fact that Asia is growing economically at 400 or 500 percent the pace of the developed West, will finance move to the East?

The answer is less than straightforward. Obviously, moving an activity from New York to London requires some but not much cultural adjustment, given the similarities in language, law, and business culture. A few former British colonial centers such as Hong Kong and Singapore offer some of these advantages, as well as relatively benign regulators and tax authorities. They also have strong professional-service infrastructures, well-educated populations, and close proximity and good travel connections to China and the rest of Asia. There is no reason that financial specialists such as hedge fund and asset managers will not pull up stakes and relocate to these centers, or that global banks will not move proprietary trading into Asian vehicles over time if things get uncomfortable enough in London and New York. However, financial centers are social constructs and seem to require a critical mass of like-minded people interacting both professionally and socially to achieve primacy. This takes a very long time, with the financial primacy of a city often occurring after the country it is located in has been overtaken by rivals.

Cultural Differences in Financial Systems

Financial depth—the stock market capitalization and outstanding-debt relative to GDP—is a used by the McKinsey Global Institute (MGI) in tracking global capital markets. Overall, the world's financial stock, equity and debt, was $212 trillion, about three times global output, in 2010. However, the financial depth of rich, developed countries averaged 427 percent (462 percent for the United States) and that of the emerging markets 197 percent (161 percent excluding China).

Now, China and India have both seen their financial stock expand by a compound annual growth rate of 20 percent or more since 2000, while the US and Europe have managed a bit over 5 percent and Japan half of that. But this is not a mechanically predictable race to financial primacy. The shape of a financial market and the skills and institutions it has accumulated over time matter more than brute depth.

In the United States, only 10 percent of the total financial stock consists of loans on the books of banks, while the bond market accounts for 48 percent, asset securitization 16 percent, and equities 26 percent. The US, following its UK roots but going well beyond them, has historically had a "market-centric" financial system, in contrast to the historically "bank-centric" financial systems of Europe and Japan (to use terms that economist Matthew Saal and I coined in a 1998 paper for the Institute of International Finance, "A Perspective on Risk and Regulatory Implications of Market Centric Financial Systems").

Bank loans are 28 percent and 23 percent of the financial stock of Europe and Japan, respectively, and their bond and equity markets are correspondingly smaller, with asset securitization markets at 4 or 5 percent. In China, bank loans account for fully 45 percent of the total financial stock. In India and the rest of Asia, the number is 30 percent. In all these cases, domestic bond markets are limited, especially for private-sector borrowers, and money markets are underdeveloped.

It may appear to be a mere matter of time for the models to converge, but they haven't since the 19th century except during the high point of New Deal financial repression in the in the United States. A bank-centric system can be used as a captive house bank by powerful corporations and conglomerates (as in Germany and Japan), or as a mechanism to direct capital to political purposes, as in China and other developing countries. Market-centric systems are dynamic and innovative because they are profit driven and objective. They don't mix well with state capitalism or crony capitalism, both systems many of these countries are comfortable with and frankly have been extraordinarily successful with of late compared to the market-centric model.

Finance may want to move to Asia, but it is an open question how welcome it would be there. Time will tell.

Why the United States Is Losing Clout but Remains Indispensable

Philip Coggan, the markets editor of the *Economist* newspaper, just published a timely book called *Paper Promises* (PublicAffairs, 2012). It argues that a system of credit-based fiat money always collapses when it becomes clear to participants that debts cannot be paid or even serviced. These crises have occurred roughly every 40 years since the invention of paper or credit money in the 17th century. The Nixon administration created a global era of fiat money by scrapping the Bretton Woods system and the last link to gold exactly 40 years ago. This gave us 40 years of global economic expansion punctuated by credit bubbles and financial crises as nation states abused their ability to create money out of thin air to finance growth. The timing is now perfect for an epic global debt crisis.

In Coggan's view, which somewhat mirrors Chapter 1 of this book, the self-indulgent "welfare states" of the European Union have arrived at this precipice first and most desperately through the folly of creating a fiat currency without a state or a lender of last resort, in the hope that the pooling of currencies would eventually force a pooling of sovereignty. They may well get the worst of both worlds: more unaccountable power in Brussels and growth-killing austerity in the unlikely event the euro is saved. The situation in the United States is less dire, but only slightly. The United States is trying to catch up with Europe in creating unaffordable social entitlements funded by debt even as the consequences of this for Europe become clearer by the day. Nobody believes this is sustainable.

To be fair, the investors and bankers also appear delusional: equity markets rally at every hint of a political fix, and then swoon when there is no fix. Nor is it possible to predict the exact path events will take, though Coggan argues that the debt hangover accumulated over the last 40 years can only be resolved by some combination of "inflation, stagnation and default," which will drive a crisis "at least as severe as the one in 2008." I would bet on financial repression.

It is probably accurate to say the last crisis never really ended. We have argued that the world is simply entering the second phase of an economic meltdown along the lines suffered in the 1930s, and the odds of the euro zone not imploding and taking the Western banking system to the brink with it are lengthening.

Coggan observes that the interests of debtors and creditors are always fundamentally at odds. Politics, both domestic and international, revolve around this conflict as much as around the rich vs. poor divide that goes back to Aristotle. As long as they can vindicate their interests politically and militarily (as the Italian bankers of the Renaissance often could not), the greatest creditors will always control the financial system. This in turn supports political hegemony, as Niall Ferguson ably points out in *The Cash Nexus* (Basic Books, 2002), which calibrates geopolitical power with financial ascendancy over three centuries.

Britain effectively led the world, including its former colony the United States, for a century after the defeat of Napoleon because the global financial system revolved around the City of London, the pound sterling, and the gold standard. The US used the British need for finance in both World Wars to undermine British global financial leadership and led the world through a dollar-based financial system after 1945. Unlike the British, however, the Americans often displayed scant regard for the interests of the global system as a whole when domestic politics were in play. Like its sterling predecessor, the dollar-centric financial system will likely take a long time to die. But the post-1945 US financial hegemony seems on the road to oblivion. (By contrast, the collapse of the euro may be quite sudden, given its fundamental economic illogic.)

Why There Is No Alternative

A new global financial system will need to be built, and many, including Coggan, think that China will be the country around which it revolves, simply because it is the world's largest creditor. This is not to downplay the challenges China faces in achieving sustainable development. However, in a global collapse of market confidence in "paper promises," the relatively limited role of market forces in China's planned economy will provide real advantages, as does the absence of electoral politics. Its ability to conduct what was probably the largest fiscal stimulus in history was central to China's weathering the first wave of the crisis in 2008–2009. In any case, China will emerge as the world's greatest creditor, even if many of its claims have been devalued. China will be like the United States after the Second World War—the last man standing—and its displacement of US global economic leadership will be accelerated whether it wants it or not. Or will China really boldly step into America's shoes? We should not bet on it.

China has always been the world's largest state, and up until 1820, it was the world's largest economy, a position it is on track to recapture by 2025 but potentially as soon as 2018. However, there is a fundamental difference that is often overlooked between China then and China now. Dynastic China was a relatively self-contained tributary empire with minimal or no need of trade beyond its borders and client states. Hence, the Chinese dismissal of the first British attempts to open trade under Lord Macartney's diplomatic mission of 1792–1794 was entirely rational because China didn't need to trade (much less finance) outside its borders.

The British Empire by contrast was a merchant-state, where trade, finance, and diplomatic influence vastly outweighed territory or military power. The United States was originally part of that empire and essentially remains a merchant-state, but an inward-looking one, given its vast internal market. Modern China is, whether it likes it or not, a merchant-state built on globalization, just as the British Empire was during the first great age of globalization it led from 1815 to 1914. This global merchant-state role is totally new to China as first a self-contained empire and then a victim of predatory merchant-states such as Britain and Japan. It is a delicate position for China to occupy, both because it is outside prior Chinese experience and because of the reactions of other countries.

The reality of China's global economic power is overshadowed by Western people's sudden consciousness of it and tendency to exaggerate it, something the same countries did concerning Japan in the 1980s. The fear and resentment of China's rise among ordinary people and political leaders in the declining countries of the West is already too much for comfort. The risk is that acceleration of Western decline and relative Chinese ascendancy in the wake of a second devastating financial meltdown could easily lead to a mutually destructive backlash, especially if China does not mitigate the dread it inspires. China is more likely to seek to integrate itself into existing global economic bodies and structures than to seek leadership, a posture ascendant Japan generally followed in the 1980s.

Another way to think about it is this: a merchant-state, drawing its power from the growth of global markets and commerce, has very different requirements for success than a power-state, where internal control and projection of military capability are paramount success factors. Since 1945, the United States has been a bit of both, while the European Union represents an abortive effort at a pure merchant empire: all soft power and no hard power. China as a rising power also needs to be a bit of both. But in doing so, China is likely to copy the tactic the Americans employed during their rise to economic primacy. That is to play the role of free rider on the US-centric financial system for as long as possible while seeking to maximize its own interests within the existing rules.

Why the System Needs a Hegemon

The great economic historian Charles Kindleberger, in writing about the causes of the Great Depression in *The World in Depression: 1929–1939* (University of

California Press, 1973), argued that every global financial system requires a "hegemon" to insure its stability and enforce its rules of conduct. The hegemon is not a global dictator, but rather a state that can influence global events. This is an expensive proposition, because for a financial hegemon to achieve success, it needs to be seen as a provider of public goods that make its hegemony acceptable if not liked by the other powers, even if this means assuming burdens for others without a direct return. For Victorian Britain, this was freedom of navigation, free trade, the rule of law, property rights, and the gold standard. These conditions required Britain to defend them, occasionally by arms, but taken together they facilitated the easy movement of goods and capital that made the Victorian era the greatest single period of economic advancement in history. This did not make historic rivals such as France, Russia, and the United States like British hegemony, but it made them amenable to it. Arguably, the failure to understand this fundamental wisdom caused the rising powers of the early 20th century, Germany and Japan, to set off the rivalries that led to their encirclement and eventual global war.

When after that conflict the US emerged as the hegemon in the global economy and politics, it took care to construct what at least had the appearance of a multilateral global governance structure. This includes the United Nations, the IMF, and World Bank, GATT (now the WTO), the OECD, BIS, and much else. These institutions have often proved vexing to certain Americans, but overall have served US interests well through their global legitimacy. One especially important area in which US norms have prevailed is the emergence of global capital markets, and with them came a market-centric model of finance that has fueled much of the economic growth and entrepreneurship of the last 20 years in both developed and emerging markets, especially Asia.

Will China Stand Up?

China has reversed a 200-year decline relative to the West in two generations, an unprecedented feat, by becoming workshop to the world and the leading exporter of goods and importer of raw materials. It has done so by a combination of massive infrastructure spending and urbanization, bringing the productive capacities of hundreds of millions of people into the global marketplace under conditions of open global trade and financial markets largely fostered by the United States and European Union. The limits of this export-driven model was clearly recognized in the latest five-year plan, which seeks to rebalance the export-driven growth model that has driven progress up to now, but at an increasing cost to social harmony. The time necessary for the envisioned transition is very limited given the impact of the crisis on Western demand and the shaky position of the Western credit system and fiat currencies, not to mention political support for globalization. Nobody has a bigger stake in the global financial system. But will it take up the role of its hegemon?

It is in fact likely that China, despite being the world's largest exporter and creditor, will for some time at least contrive to avoid the role of hegemon, especially the burden of reserve currency issuer and lender of last resort. Reserve currencies, with the pound sterling as the most successful to date, become a global benchmark and safe haven that drives up their value relative to other currencies, which in many circumstances damages export competitiveness. Japan, the very model of an export-driven economy, remains the world's largest creditor, with overseas assets of nearly $7 trillion. It has never aspired to financial hegemony, since it has been able to take advantage of public goods provided by America, the world's largest debtor.

The lessons from the rise of the United States to global economic primacy (America overtook the UK economy in size around 1879) are instructive. A key to US economic success was being a relatively benign free rider on the world economic order created and supported by Britain. This allowed American business and finance to focus on the development of its vast domestic market. America leveraged the global financial system built up by Britain around strong institutions, including free trade and capital movement, the Bank of England, sterling linked to the gold standard, settlement of international trade through bills on London (i.e., the pound as currency of clearing and settlement for all cross-border transactions), and the largest and deepest money and capital markets, all backed by the English common law and its respect for contract and property rights. From 1865 to 1914, most of the capital to build the US industrial base and infrastructure was raised in London, and American trade was financed and external claims were settled in sterling. America only briefly joined the gold standard, but instead pursued a liberal (as in loose) domestic credit system based on fractional reserve banking, and until 1913 eschewed the discipline of central banking.

Britain accepted and even clung to the burden of maintaining a reserve currency until forced to impose strict exchange controls at the outbreak of war in 1939 largely through its governing class's confusion between national prestige and practical economics. After the war, the "temporary" exchange controls stayed on until 1979. Sterling's role as a reserve currency was unsustainable. The dollar became by default the only potential reserve currency after the war, but the remarkable fact is that by the 1944 Bretton Woods conference, the United States had been the largest economy in the world for about 65 years without taking up the burden of financial hegemon. In fact, the lack of a hegemon with the means to lead the global financial system effectively was one of the underlying conditions that led to the extended global slump between the wars, since America lacked the will and skill to play the role, and Britain had lost its overseas portfolio of investments and had fallen deeply into debt.

The Alexandrine Greek poet Cavafy wrote a famous poem, "Waiting for the Barbarians," in which the inhabitants of an unnamed empire assemble in the forum to greet the barbarians who are due to arrive. The poem ends with the despair of the inhabitants when they realize the barbarians are not coming to relieve them of the burdens of civilization. America needs to buck up and realize that neither China nor any other power has the will or depth of skill and experience to play international financial hegemon for the foreseeable future, even if America's circumstances feel much reduced at the moment. As a practical matter, not only does America remain the indispensable anchor of the global financial system, but its citizens have in their power the capacity to learn from the excesses that led to the 2008 crisis and do better going forward.

The next section of this book will address how we can positively adjust to the world after finance. Chapter 6 addresses the need for consumers to learn to live without easy credit, and Chapter 7 lays out a path for the fundamental reconstruction of the financial services industry itself.

The Consumer in the World After Finance

Living Within Our Means

The notion of defining human beings as consumers is very American and very recent. For all of history up to the 20th century, men and women were primarily defined as producers. We see this in surnames such as Taylor, Weaver, and Smith. Before production and daily life became divorced by industrial organization and urban life, only a small elite of landholders and officers of church and state were in any sense consumers of anything but the staples of life. Most people worked to survive and little else, and generation after generation lived the same way their forebears did.

Two things changed all that: the New World with its bounty of resources to be seized by the adventurous and ruthless, and "the lever of riches," to use historian Joel Mokyr's happy phrase for his study of technological creativity and economic progress. The advent of technologies that substituted carbon energy for muscle vastly increased the product of industry. Improvement in physical and information logistics—the ability to move goods and information—revolutionized commerce. As a result, living standards everywhere in the West, but especially in the vast space of North America, were set on a course of constant improvement after millennia of stagnation. Each generation could confidently expect their children to have more than they enjoyed in terms of material well-being, all things being equal. Even those who suffered misfortune and financial ruin could reasonably hope for a better life for their children and grandchildren. This, probably more than any urge for freedom in a political sense, made America a magnet for the masses of the Old World, where the benefits of progress were less dramatic and far less widely distributed.

There is a phrase that long had meaning in Britain but lost its meaning in America: one's *station in life*. Europe, and indeed all old civilizations, assumed and to an extent enforced fixed status or class positions for people. Hankering after things reserved for one's betters was a vice. Living sober, respectable lives appropriate to one's station meant "living within one's means." Thrift was both a virtue and a necessity. Debt was an evil and fraught with peril, both moral and legal. As an old British marching song of the American Revolutionary War put it:

> *In Carlow town I lived, I own,*
> All free from debt and dangers,
> *Till Colonel Reilley listed me*
> *To join the Wicklow Rangers*

"Free from debt and dangers" describes the past happy state of the soldier before becoming a Redcoat. Debt and danger were equivalent and best avoided.

Niall Ferguson, as noted in Chapter 2, names consumerism as one of the "killer apps" that made Western civilization the dominant force in modern history. Consumerism in Ferguson's telling largely revolves around cotton manufacture and blue jeans. The reason Ferguson gives for its pivotal role is that mass consumption is precisely what made industrialization worth it. When consumers were confined to the old upper classes, handcrafted luxury goods were the products that mattered. If you build and run an enormous cotton mill, you need vast numbers of people to buy cotton cloth and the clothes made from it. These people did appear in large enough numbers to make textiles the leading sector of the industrial revolution everywhere from Manchester, England, to Manchester, New Hampshire, to Japan.

The people who flocked to buy cheap cotton goods were the first consumers, driven by the desire to have things beyond their station in life. When cotton was a scarce luxury from India and Egypt, ladies of quality wore muslin gowns in the summer. When average men and women aspired to comfortable cotton clothes in place of homespun linen and wool, they created a mass market for mass production. This provided employment and wages that allowed the range of mass-market goods to expand. Mass-market pottery made its way into every home. More people could afford homes, as consumption drove employment, which fueled more consumption.

The Great Depression and World War II put a damper on this upward spiral, but only for a brief span of time. Pent-up demand for consumer goods and housing helped fuel the postwar boom in America and, later, Western Europe. However, this demand was not generated just with cash wages and the spending down of forced wartime savings. It was built on credit.

The Money of the Mind

Credit is an essential aspect of business-to-business commerce because there is always a timing gap between making things that cost money for labor and materials and selling them. In overseas trade, the time and money involved could be considerable, so providing the money became a specialized activity we call banking. For centuries, banking only existed to provide "working capital" to grease the wheels of commerce. Loans were meant to be "self-liquidating," meaning that the money advanced would be used to generate the income the borrower needed to repay it. For example, if a store has a need to stock up on goods before Christmas, lending it the money to do so is sound banking if the store has a track record of good Christmas sales. Lending people money so they can go shopping for Christmas presents is not, strictly speaking, banking at all. There is nothing in the transaction to generate income. Lending people money essentially so they can spend it without generating wealth has of course always existed, but banks normally didn't do it; moneylenders did. People were expected to save up the money they needed for Christmas, which is why banks invented so-called Christmas clubs. Merchants, both big department stores and local shops, have always allowed good customers to buy things on credit. Sending an important person a bill instead of demanding payment was a common practice. Even before the First World War, merchants were formalizing these practices into "charge accounts" to boost sales.

James Grant, in his classic *Money of the Mind* (Farrar, Straus and Giroux, 1995), traces how Americans—the things described here went much further, earlier, in the United States than elsewhere—"democratized" credit and overturned classic lending standards beginning in the 1920s. Louis Hyman's previously mentioned *Debtor Nation* traces the development of a consumer credit "infrastructure" by trial and error in the postwar era. In Chapter 2, I told how banks went down the primrose path of consumer banking in response to losing their traditional corporate business to the capital markets. The point here is that a robust and growing consumer finance infrastructure grew up with the postwar boom to get Americans homes, cars, and appliances without saving up for them. Installment credit, car loans, and charge accounts became more available than ever. So did home mortgages, with considerable government intervention ranging from guarantees and subsidies to income tax deductions for mortgage interest. In the process, credit morphed from something personal between the consumer and the lender, be it a store or a savings-and-loan company, to being objective and mechanical.

In Hyman's telling, this was a reaction to discrimination that excluded African Americans and others from consumer credit, which somewhat amazingly had in America come to be seen as a right, not the privilege it had been and remains in most societies. Fair-lending laws forced the expanding consumer credit universe to "legitimize" its practices by creating objective criteria for making credit decisions. That is probably true enough, but as I note in Chapter 2, the banks themselves had ample reasons to turn credit into a business with national scale and scope. This by definition meant they could not, like generations of lenders before them, base their credit decisions on the character and life circumstances of people they actually knew. Objective, neutral credit decisions were needed for both justice and efficiency.

The Credit Score

The net result was the invention of the credit score, a number that represents how risky a consumer is relative to all other consumers. Credit scores are more deeply ingrained in the consumer finance world of America than in any other society. They require that consumers allow a number of private bureaus to collect and analyze information on the amount of credit they have outstanding, as well as their income and employment status and history, and whether or not they pay their bills on time. While some sensitive information is excluded from credit scoring by law, the amount of information that is collected is extraordinary. Many foreign jurisdictions have privacy laws that would permit far less information to be harvested and gleaned. However, most Americans, including politicians and regulators for the most part, have an instinctual understanding that the system of credit reporting is the price society pays for broad access to consumer credit. Americans make this trade-off with limited fair-credit-reporting protections, while many other societies do not.

It is critical to understand that a credit score is only a measure of whether a consumer can service a certain amount of credit—that is, make timely interest and principal payments. It is not concerned with the ability to pay off debts over time. What it really measures is the probability that an individual will default. This is a statistical model–based determination, and as such is hostage to historical experience of the behavior of tens of millions of individuals. The factors that over time have proved most predictive include not only behavior—late or missed payments on any bill, not just a loan, signals potential default—but also circumstances. Home ownership of long duration is a plus. So is long-term employment at the same firm.

The credit score also allows the whole machinery of "securitized credit," the bundling of consumer loans into securities, to operate. Vast numbers of consumer loans and mortgages can be mingled into packages, or *tranches*, based on credit score. This, of course, was a key flaw in the markets leading up to the 2008 market meltdown. The investment bankers thought they had the machinery and models to turn low-credit-score loans into Triple A securities. The crisis proved that the models and structures were deeply flawed in many cases. But the credit score itself suffers from the same basic limitation as all statistical efforts to predict the future based on history. Sometimes, to borrow from Yogi Berra, "The future ain't what it used to be." For the entire period when credit scores were being developed into objective predictive tools to measure the risk of default, the United States was enjoying what I've been calling the Great Moderation. Between 1982 and 2008 there had been a steady rise in asset prices, especially for homes, and job creation was robust enough to keep unemployment reasonably low. There was plenty of turnover in the US job market and some painful restructuring in many industries, but long-term unemployment was not a feature of American life. Together, this meant that ownership of a home and employment history were highly predictive of default risk. The Panic of 2008 and the policy response to it have undermined both the value of homes and the nature of the labor market in fundamental ways. The "infrastructure" of mass consumer credit has yet to adjust to the new reality.

Employment and Consumer Credit

Americans tend to think of unemployment as something that is a temporary aberration from the norm of stable, full-time work. It occurs for two reasons: people are let go when companies hit bad times or fail, but people also quit their jobs in expectation of finding something better when times are good. The United States, relative to other industrial countries, has historically maintained a liberal and flexible labor market where millions of jobs were created and destroyed each year. This high level of churn in the labor market meant that although long-term employment with one firm—the norm for middle- and upper-working-class people for a generation after World War II—was in decline, people with a strong work history were a good bet to stay employed most of the time. Obviously, this is critical to the validity of credit scores and thus the whole consumer credit system. Building up and maintaining a good credit history was widely understood to be a key to the good life in a credit-driven economy. If people could earn enough to service their mortgages, car loans, and credit card balances, they would. If the private sector created a steady stream of new businesses, something that is baked into the so-called birth-death model used in government employment statistics, lending against future income was a good bet.

For the most part, this was a bet that few other financial systems were willing to take—not that there was no consumer finance in places such as France and Germany, but that it was either retailer installment credit for large-ticket items or overdraft credit tightly linked to current income flowing by direct deposit into the same current account. This system limited credit to a small multiple of monthly salary to help bank customers smooth out their cash flow, rather than substituting borrowing for income. The American consumer credit model assumed a degree of income growth and increased ability to service debt over time—something that seemed justified by experience with dynamic, mobile labor markets with little structural unemployment.

Structural Unemployment: Insiders and Outsiders

The structure of employment in most other countries is different from that of pre-2008 America. Labor markets in Europe especially are very rigid compared to the United States, because of both high levels of unionization and very strong laws protecting workers from being fired once taken into employment. Further, high "social charges" on employers for things such as health care makes hiring full-time help a very risky and expensive proposition. The net result is a three-tiered system in which an elite and politically powerful group of "insider" workers in government and large firms enjoy almost absolute job security, generous wages and benefits, long vacations, and early retirements. The second tier of workers are a byproduct of the first, since companies are reluctant to take chances on hiring anyone who is not either connected to insiders or an insider somewhere else. Most young people are neither, so they work in temporary positions, small businesses, or the "shadow economy" of unregulated (though not necessarily illegal) activities.

In countries such as Italy and France, the chance for these outsiders to become insiders is very small, but the liberalization of labor markets needed to change this is politically toxic. Below the outsiders, large swaths of the working-age population live on government assistance programs, partially because benefits are generous enough to make such a life about as comfortable as the employed life of the outsiders with far less effort. A statistic called the *labor force participation rate* is telling. In the United States before 2008, this often ran as high as 68 percent, meaning that the nearly seven out of ten adults below retirement age were in the labor market. By contrast, many European countries had only between five and six out of ten adults working. The rest lived off the state or in the shadows. Of course, this structure is only possible because the insiders paid very high direct taxes (so called value-added taxes of 20 percent or more are common) and income taxes at rates well above US levels. This in turn depressed entrepreneurial activity and economic dynamism, reinforcing the jobs-creation deficit; but until the unfolding European debt crisis showed that the system could not be sustained, many Europeans felt their system to be more just and civilized than "liberalism" or "Anglo-Saxon" free-market capitalism. The term *solidarity* is often evoked in Europe as the moral foundation of this economic and social setup.

Since 2008, the United States has swung toward the European model for two reasons. The first and probably least important was the election of a government that finds it attractive on grounds of "fairness," something akin to solidarity. America remains too much of a center-right country for that tendency to go uncontested, as the congressional election of 2010 proved, so the political system remains gridlocked. The second and more intractable reason is that a long, disguised drift toward structural unemployment has become a riptide.

The Hollowing Out of America

The credit-fueled consumption and growth of the quarter-century leading up to the crisis obscured a profound hollowing out of the American economy. The two leading causes of this are the collapse of the Communist experiment and its imitators across the developing world on one hand and a powerful new wave of technological progress on the other. For mankind as a whole, these have been very good things. Of the world's seven billion people, only a few tens of millions live cut off from the global economy in holdout states such as North Korea and Cuba. Before the collapse of the Soviet Union and, earlier and more significant, Deng's bold reforms in China, over half of mankind had no access to markets for their labor and talents. This effectively sheltered American, European, and Japanese labor from the rigors of global competition, except of course between each other.

Today, workers across the globe find themselves in competition with each other. Work will migrate to where enterprises find the best combination of costs, skills, and flexibility. That is why nearly half the world's manufacturing output is now in greater China. The result is that perhaps a billion people can now lead basic middle-class lives in the so-called BRIC countries of Brazil, Russia, India, and China, places that scarcely had a middle class a generation ago. Overall, this means that the global economic pie is getting larger rapidly, but the share enjoyed by Western consumers is not growing. In their role as producers and wage earners, American and other Western workers are still vastly too costly for firms facing global competition to employ them. Don't be misled by the election-year rhetoric of wicked corporations shipping American jobs overseas and promises to do something about it. The jobs are not coming back, ever.

The reason for this is that the real job killer is that lever of riches, technological innovation. This is of course a very old story. The first wave of industrialization destroyed the livelihood of traditional cloth workers from England to India and China. In 1790, the first US census showed four-fifths of the population engaged in agriculture. Technology destroyed all those jobs, but it replaced them with far more remunerative work in industry and services— jobs that didn't exist until new technologies called them into being. Economic optimists argue that after a period of adjustment, this will happen again as innovative entrepreneurs lever the productivity of new technologies into better, higher-paying jobs.

The problem this time around is that relentless global competition is forcing enterprises to lower their costs of production (and not incidentally, improve quality) by all means possible. Advanced manufacturing technology combining computers, sensors, and robots does both and is rapidly improving and being deployed worldwide. The classic argument that automation-driven productivity gains translate into higher wages and living standards may no longer hold. US manufacturing output has in fact held up reasonably well, growing from around $1.2 trillion to $2.2 trillion between 1980 and 2010 when measured in dollars at their 2005 value. This has not translated into employment numbers or wages, which continue to be repressed by global competition. Over the same period, the United States lost over 7 million jobs in manufacturing, and continued shrinkage is projected for 2010 through 2020 by the US Department of Labor. The review article "Back in the Game" by Ed Crooks and Hal Weitzman (*Financial Times*, February 10, 2012) on the comeback of the US manufacturing industry—heralded by Clint Eastwood in his controversial "Halftime in America" Super Bowl commercial—sums things up as follows: "The comeback of US manufacturing is real but it will never again create prosperous middle-class cities such as 1950s Detroit. There is no conceivable manufacturing revival that will bring back all the jobs that have gone."

Unless the United States cuts itself off from the global economy—a populist prescription for much of our history, but an unrealistic one—real wages will have to adjust to global norms. If a steady job does not produce a middle-class income capable of servicing debt, the entire edifice of consumer credit becomes untenable at best and the road to debt peonage at worst.

The New Reality

So what does this mean for you as an individual, especially if you are unlucky enough to be entering the labor market at this time? The logic of the three-tier European-style labor market seems to be winning. For those who work in activities that have no market-competitive dimension, insider status is for the moment assured. Unionized public-service employees have begun to pull ahead of their private-sector counterparts in wages, especially hourly wages, benefits, and pensions. This has long been the case in places such as France and Quebec, where 60 percent or so of the population, including the best educated, work for the state in absolute job security. Employment in large enterprises that are politically connected, such as the bailed-out Detroit automakers, is obviously somewhat shakier. As the government exerts more political control over health care, finance, and energy in the United States, the circle of privileged insider employees in firms subsidized or otherwise favored by the state is likely to expand somewhat. Subsidy-based industries such as "alternative energy," however, have thus far not produced the employment expected and remain on the cusp of the inner circle. Infrastructure projects, which at least should have a completion date, are probably not capable of sustaining insider employment status, but their ongoing maintenance and operations often can.

The outsiders pay for the insiders in two ways. The obvious one is paying ever-higher shares of their income in tax to government at all levels, but the more insidious is through the mechanism I focused on in Chapter 4, financial repression. In a perfect free market, credit and investment would be allocated through a mixture of fear and greed. Super-safe government debt would attract its fair share of people's investment spending, directly and through institutional investors such as pension funds, but would have to pay market rates in competition with other users of money in the private sector. If the state and its corporate allies get to rig the system, as they have always done in most countries, entrepreneurs and small businesses will get squeezed out because the return on lending to and investing in new businesses and small business expansions will not be enough to satisfy greed.

Since private-sector employment is closely linked to the birth of new companies, both in reality and in government models, employment opportunities for outsiders will suffer. Both Western Europe and Japan have a vast shortfall in financing for small and medium-sized businesses, and a near-total absence of financing for entrepreneurs and startups. The United States used to be an exception, which is why it created tens of millions of net jobs between the 1980s and 2008, while Europe and Japan produced very few net new jobs outside of government. Overall, US job growth in the pre-crisis decades ran at about 1.5 percent a year while continental Europe managed only 0.5 percent. Over time, a 1 percent gap is huge, amounting to millions of jobs a year. The creation of new employers, especially in services, through entrepreneurship, was a key to American performance in this regard. Now Americans have joined the Old World club, multiplying the nonfinancial obstacles to private business through regulatory and tax burdens equal to or greater than those in the Old World. This almost guarantees a widening gap between the economic prospects of insiders and outsiders. However, from the self-interested view of the state and its insider clients, this cements their power and privilege.

The End of Employment

The need to take care of those who will never have a real chance at steady employment is a reality no one can flinch from accepting. The question is, can they be helped to be productive and independent or are they to be kept dependent on state largesse? For continental Europe, a relatively generous social safety net has been the answer throughout the postwar period, especially since the 1960s. Here again, America was an exception. The substantial expansion of the welfare state embodied in the so-called Great Society was seen to produce long-term dependency and social dysfunction by a broad range of observers during the 1990s. This consensus led to the landmark welfare reforms of that decade. However, that was against the background of an economic boom driven by the financial economy, a "dot-com" bubble in new technologies, and pro-market reforms of the 1980s. Record labor-force participation during the dot-com boom made the so-called "welfare to work" requirements embedded in the reforms aimed at limiting the time people could receive benefits without seeking work or training appear feasible and in the best interest of people mired in poverty. Indeed, welfare rolls fell sharply in the boom economy of the 1990s.

The picture today could scarcely be more different. Labor-force participation rates have fallen to levels not seen in over three decades—down to 64 percent from 67.4 percent—with perhaps one potential worker in five unemployed or underemployed. These realities are hidden from the public by the perverse way the Bureau of Labor Statistics calculates unemployment, which is based only on persons actively seeking work during the survey period.

On this basis, US unemployment fell to 8.3 percent in January 2012, eliciting much upbeat comment; however, the Gallup polling organization puts unemployment at 9.1 percent. When combined with part-time workers seeking full-time work, Gallup estimates an underemployment rate of 19.3 percent. The number of long-term unemployed—those without a job for 27 weeks or more—remains stubbornly unchanged at around 5.5 million, some 42.9 percent of all unemployed.

Against this reality, politicians across the spectrum have been either eagerly or reluctantly shedding the pretense that unemployment assistance is a short-term insurance scheme supported by premiums paid by workers and employers. When benefits are extended to 99 weeks, it becomes an outright dole system and eventually an entitlement to permanent income support. The myth that Social Security, the most popular and enduring of New Deal innovations, was a contributory pension scheme rather than a form of welfare is being exposed by repeated (and what may eventually be permanent) payroll tax holidays. Universal and mandatory health insurance is another massive wealth transfer that creates a disincentive to job creation, as 70 years of European experience attests; but once in place, such systems are impossible to reform, much less cut, as UK experience amply illustrates.

The net results of all these developments are that a new elite of insiders are doing very well and the lot of the displaced working class is being attended to, but the vast majority of outsiders laboring in the private sector are caught in the same squeeze that their counterparts in Europe have known for generations. If they work in a job or calling subject to global competition—a category being widely and rapidly expanded by digital communications to embrace even more high-value activities such as law and medical diagnosis—their real incomes will be held static or decline. If they work in the non-tradable private sector, which includes the learned professions as well as jobs in personal services, health care, retailing, and construction, they face the impacts of mounting regulation and taxation. If they are retired, they face confiscation of their savings by financial repression and ever rising property taxes to pay public-sector employees and public pension schemes. Property taxes above a certain threshold are, as is too little noted, a form of confiscation of the real property of homeowners, especially those on fixed incomes.

If this sounds bleak, it is. Most Europeans have been resigned to such a system for a very long time. They are not entirely unhappy with the trade-offs, especially if they are insiders. Taxes are high, but not too hard to evade, and things like health care and higher education are free if not especially high in quality. Unlike outsiders, the insiders have high levels of economic security and ample leisure. The outsiders may be resentful, but lack the political clout to do anything except cast the occasional protest vote for ultranationalist politicians such as the Le Pens in France. The excluded who live on the dole can burn cars or riot occasionally, as we saw in the United Kingdom in the summer of 2011 (and we see in France habitually), but they have even less influence over their lives. Nobody really expects to live better than the previous generation in these societies. Americans once took the hope of a better life for their kids as part of their civic faith. Increasing numbers now expect the opposite. Resignation to declining prospects has not historically been an American trait, but it is becoming one.

Innovation and Education Will Save America

As little as a decade ago, it seemed inconceivable that America was ever going to accept a less prosperous future. People from all over the world came (and still come) to America with the hope of making their fortune or at least giving their children a better life. In America, the ability to start up a business in a garage and change the world once seemed normal. America had the best universities and created masters of innovation. As Bill Gates and Steve Jobs, among others, illustrated, America was the land of infinite possibilities for bold entrepreneurial talent. As the improbable global success of the iPod and Facebook illustrates, America's innovation edge is still there. The problem is that much of the innovation in digital technology does not translate into mass employment opportunities for the workforce that America has available. Apple is a global icon only America could produce. But its brilliant gadgets are made in China for the most part. Some of this comes down to cost and some to lack of skilled and diligent workers, but above all, to the lack of production-level engineers (as opposed to brilliant designers, where the United States still has an edge) in a country with the world's best schools of engineering.

The two most common solutions put forth for putting America back on track for renewed prosperity and raising living standards are innovation and education. Politicians of all persuasions, business leaders, and pundits all agree these are the secret sauce, however much they may disagree on other issues, such as taxes and the scope of government. Education and innovation are, of course, linked, insofar as innovation is more likely to be expected in a highly educated workforce. Also, without venture capital and other financial risk-takers in dynamic and deep capital markets, innovation is unlikely to achieve the scope and scale required for commercial viability. This is why so much brilliant British technology, from jet propulsion to penicillin, only became viable when taken over by American firms. Countries that have tried to foster innovation with state subsidies and so-called industrial policy have a poor track record as well, with the US attempt to will alternative energy into commercial viability a case in point. Most innovation fails because it doesn't deliver economic value to customers that justifies its deployment. Value is ultimately a market judgment. It is almost impossible to predict and make bets on successful innovation.

For example, much to the horror of the green movement, domestic oil and natural gas are enjoying a renaissance in America—and not so much despite political and regulatory hostility but because of it. Innovative new drilling and extraction techniques probably would not have been developed if so many obstacles had not been imposed on where energy companies could drill conventional wells. As discussed in Chapter 2, the securitization of retail credit was a reaction to financial regulation, which historically has always been a key driver of financial innovation. The very randomness and perverseness of innovation means that "experts" spending public money (or big public companies spending their shareholders' funds) are more likely than not to get it wrong, and very greedy but not-very-expert venture capitalists making random bets are more likely to get it right. The process isn't pretty, and lots of money is wasted, but adequate rewards for financial risk-takers are probably as important to viable innovation as science and engineering, and perhaps more so. This was perhaps the greatest advantage the American economy had before the crisis. It is now at risk, as the very legitimacy of institutions such as Bain Capital is called into question from all sides. Economically effective innovation and a robust and free-capital market full of risk-takers are joined at the hip. We cannot hope for one while repressing the other.

The Education Bubble

If innovation is not a silver bullet for reversing the decline of American living standards, more and better education must be part of any answer. Very few voices can be found to oppose the notion that education is an unalloyed good. In some quarters, the percentage of youths in post-secondary education is viewed as a gauge of national competitiveness. The truth of the matter, however, is far more complex. While there is a lifetime earnings gap between people with college degrees and those without, the link between the credential and income is still ambiguous (except in the case of few hard-to-obtain professional-school degrees). Fundamentally, a lazy business world uses the lack of a college degree to screen out people from jobs that could easily be done by a high-school graduate or even a dropout. This excessive worship of formal credentials instead of character and ability favors the insiders over the outsiders, but it also deprives the economy of top talent. My best boss in banking left school at 15, and most managers in UK retail banks came up from long apprenticeships as clerks and branch staff. The late Sir Dennis Weatherstone left school at 16 to become a clerk at JPMorgan in London and retired as chairman and CEO. These examples are not limited to commerce. In fact, a very successful consulting colleague of mine is the product of an apprenticeship without benefit of an academic high school. Germany's robust apprenticeship system provides a path to well-paid craft work for the majority of young people with limited academic interests or aptitude. The results are seen in the quality and continuous innovation that Germany's industries are celebrated for around the world.

Americans have always been a bit ambiguous in their attitudes about education. They want it to serve practical ends, yet they shy away from channeling the intellectually uninterested or unable majority into useful training. Formal (and compulsory) education up to high school became a government function in the 19th century in response to industrialization and immigration, essentially creating a factory system for producing tractable workers and "Americanizing" foreigners. Discipline and conformity trumped any concern with abstract learning, but basic numeracy and literacy was delivered to the system's products. A high-school diploma, held by about one in five Americans before World War II, certified a basic level of accomplishment that employers could count on.

The system has since become a ruinously expensive and highly politicized domain, incapable of producing a competitive work force and seemingly impervious to reform. Some of the loudest complaints and much of the constituency for reform comes from American business, which finds itself starved of numerate and literate workers even in a very slack labor market. Real reform is problematic in an environment that makes education a political football at every level of government. The very phrase "no child left behind" tells you something is terribly wrong. Americans insist on radically democratic and equal outcomes from the public schools, a virtual guarantee of mediocrity. Other countries' educational systems tend to be run like funnels or sieves where most children deliberately get left behind through high-stakes examinations. Only a talented and hardworking minority pursue academic subjects that lead to university. This system has its own problems, largely because the offspring of the educated and well-off insiders tend to be disproportionately successful in the exam system. But family background increases educational success and access in the United States as well, either through residence in the right suburbs or access to elite private schools.

Fundamentally, the notion that education makes people wealthier and is a route to the prosperous middle class is increasingly questionable. If one has disciplined, educated, middle-class parents, especially if blessed with an intact family, the odds of living a life similar to them are pretty good. Going to college is as much something such people do as it is a source of useful skills. It is much harder to achieve an orderly and productive life if one doesn't experience it growing up. The odds of successfully completing college are much longer for those who haven't, and the value of doing so much more ambiguous. Somewhat cruelly, vast numbers of students go to college because, as with high-school diplomas a generation ago, it is almost a necessity for employment. Others go out of conformity with their parents' expectations. In the process, they accumulate vast amounts of student loans—in round numbers, a trillion dollars, a sum larger than the amount of revolving credit card debt. The debt incurred by students continues to grow out of control simply because there is no market discipline on the price of education as long as subsidized government loans are available.

These student loans, which have effectively been nationalized, form a millstone around the financial life of the recipient for many years, distorting career choices and making it harder to finance other purchases young adults require, such as cars and homes. Many people run up these debts acquiring credentials in soft or dubious fields such as the social sciences, or degrees in subjects that accept all comers, such as communications or marketing. Unfairly or not, first-generation college students are best served acquiring a highly marketable credential if they are doing so on credit. Too many American students have a basically remedial college experience and have paid through the nose for things public secondary education should have provided but did not.

Very few Americans study really tough scientific subjects. In fact, top programs in science and engineering at the leading American research universities are overwhelmingly populated by students from the emerging markets of Asia. In poor countries, hard disciplines that lead to tangible work such as engineering and medicine are very attractive to education-hungry youths and their parents. However, unless these young people acquire the scarce few residence visas, such talent is lost to the United States, despite being a huge potential contributor to innovation and new business formation. And unfortunately, too many insider interests are threatened for there to be any real reform to address this issue.

The net result is that insider children tend to replicate their parent's success (and would, to an extent, even without their college educations, few of which have any real rigor). Outsiders are left with mountains of student debt, few marketable skills, and the prospect of long bouts of structural unemployment. Many observers believe that overinvestment in education will trigger yet another financial market panic as millions of student loans incurred acquiring dubious degrees result in defaults or government bailouts.

The New Class

Of course, if one is lucky enough to graduate from one of the 20 or so US universities that are highly selective and famous, the chances of entering into the inner sanctum of insiders is very high. One in four members of the Obama administration has some sort of Harvard degree, and the top ranks of the law, investment banking, and consulting professions are remarkably similar in education and outlook.

Of course, something similar, if less extreme, was true a century ago, when the list of hyper-elite institutions was essentially the same, led by the Ivy League colleges that mostly predate the founding of the United States. The vast majority of the 1 percent of the population that went to college before the Morrell Act of 1862 (which created public colleges on a large scale) became educated because they were already privileged. Their parents' station in life assured them that they were going to be the leaders of society in any case. As famously put by John Henry Cardinal Newman in *The Idea of a University*, the aim of a university education was not utilitarian but rather to produce a social type, the gentleman (there were no university women in the cardinal's time). The gentleman essentially justified his lofty social position by serving others rather than self-seeking. Gentlemen by definition did not work, except in the public service or in the professions. The very term *liberal arts* means subjects fit for gentlemen rather than mere merchants and mechanics. Latin, Greek, mathematics, and philosophy made the cut; engineering and agriculture did not. That is why the early land-grant colleges were often confined by their original state charters to useful subjects such as agriculture and mining. The idea of being ruled by a self-identified caste of gentlemen, something the early Federalists took for granted, was firmly rejected by democratic America, as *Empire of Liberty* (Oxford, 2009), the marvelous history of America up to 1815 by Gordon Wood, documents on many levels.

Two centuries later, we are effectively ruled in many spheres by a similar small caste formed in the same universities and a handful of others. The key distinction is that although their parents are often highly successful, the new elite educated caste—the New Class, to borrow a term from the title of Milovan Djilas's famous critique of Tito's Yugoslavia—are products of ferocious competition for the glittering prizes offered by admission to the "best" schools. They feel entitled to status and wealth gained, as they sincerely believe, through merit. This does not lead to an ethic of gentlemanly—or gentlewomanly—altruism toward outsiders. As Charles Murray documents in his recent *Coming Apart* (Crown Forum, 2012), the new meritocracy—at most 400,000 or so individuals in government, higher education, journalism, the arts, finance, and the professions—occupies a world of its own, increasingly isolated in tastes, habits, beliefs, and even physical contact from ordinary people. This is unprecedented in America, which despite massive inequality in incomes over long periods of time had always maintained a shared civic culture.

What makes this relevant to this book is that although a few thousand highly paid bankers and lawyers were displaced by the 2008 meltdown, the New Class was not much affected in terms of employment. Its members have a certain disdain for mass consumerism and the culture of consumer credit that supports it. They depend little on manufacturing and typically prefer a greener planet to blue-collar jobs. Declining living standards in a world after finance are likely to leave their gilded lives untouched. This detachment of political and cultural elites from the concerns of ordinary workers and business proprietors is profoundly unhealthy for both in the long run.

Seeking Shelter

Last year, a member of my London club, the Travellers Club, loudly complained over his postprandial brandy, "There is no damned way to make any money in Britain any more except earn it!" Just so, I thought, but we Yanks will soon be in the same boat. Before the 2008 financial market meltdown, there were plenty of ways of making money with money. With interest rates in major Western countries glued around 1 percent, it will be impossible for people to make a reasonable return on their savings unless they make risky bets on equities. In fact, reinflating the stock market and even house prices by keeping returns on savings derisory is part of the whole financial repression playbook. Policymakers, at least American ones, seem eager to reinflate the pre-crisis asset bubble. This is partially because they are trapped in a Keynesian mindset that sees the whole problem of restoring economic growth in terms of ramping back up consumer spending. Rising stock prices are meant to create a *wealth effect*—the illusion of wealth that lends people the confidence to spend and borrow. This also explains the obsessive (and to date, failed) attempts to reinflate the US housing bubble, the very root of the crisis, instead of letting it bottom out at some sort of equilibrium between supply and demand. In the United Kingdom, where supply has been severely constrained, the housing bubble has not deflated in a meaningful way, so it seems supply and demand do work after all.

The impact of low interest rates over long periods of time always and everywhere creates asset bubbles and distorts markets. The hoarding of cash by banks and corporations in part reflects the reluctance of management to play in a rigged card game with lousy stakes. However, the impacts on the financial fortunes of the average consumer concern us here. Unless a sudden return to robust growth triggers inflation by pulling all the cash-hoarders off the sidelines—an unlikely but scary thought—the new norm for households will be one in which, as my friend says, the way to make money will be salary income. And, for all the reasons we have rehearsed, income will inevitably be far more highly taxed if the insiders have any say in the matter. Since no level of taxation could possibly meet the entitlement claims of my generation (yes, I am a baby boomer, born in 1946), plus the public union pension claims in most Western countries, something will have to give. Here I would not bet against the insiders putting off the day of reckoning until things become catastrophic. Do not dismiss the possibility of wealth taxes and nationalization of private pensions in the name of fairness. Such things have happened, even in Britain.

Assuming happily that your personal wealth and pension plan are not going to be taxed, nationalized, or inflated away (real possibilities but not worth dwelling on), you will receive less income from them than you planned for and expected. Many retirement plans and financial advisors look to 8 percent returns over time on invested money. That might just be achievable with a highly selective stock portfolio where value investments were made with impeccable timing.

As likely, we could see the baby boomers, who were never great savers and put a lot of money to work in the market late in their careers, forced to cash out at any price, creating a buyer's market in stocks. This is not just a matter for individual investors, but will impact institutional investors such as insurance companies and mutual funds.

Also, don't be surprised to see annuities slashed or insurance companies fail. Most likely this will be avoided, but whatever your chosen age for retirement, it is almost certainly far too low to give you the income you planned for. Increasing life expectancy of the retired and lower real income for the shrinking number of young workers will make our pay-as-you-go unfunded entitlements, including Social Security, hard to sustain without levels of taxation that cannot conceivably be collected. Although many people expect to keep working well beyond the traditional retirement age of 65, their ability to get and keep jobs amid a sea of younger, cheaper outsiders is highly questionable. Realistically, only professionals such as doctors, lawyers, and professors are likely to have that option, along with proprietors of their own businesses.

If this sounds like the end of the world, well, it isn't. The policy errors that it assumes can in fact be avoided through a change of political direction in the next few years, something that the public has the power to effect through the electoral process. However, even if fiscal responsibility carries the day, the future will be challenging simply because the iron facts of demography—an aging population requires more services—and the need to deleverage the economy cannot be avoided. The daunting challenge is that only a radical reform of our post–World War II institutional setups can change outcomes, and that is probably beyond the art of the possible in politics unless the public demands it. As individuals, we should look to our own devices rather than political saviors of either persuasion. This requires us to re-imagine the world we will live in going forward and figure out how to make the changes in our habits and behavior that will allow us to thrive in the new circumstances. The world after finance will be a very different place.

Going Japanese

What might life in that world look like? I call it going Japanese. I spent a good deal of time in Japan in 2011, a country I greatly admire on many levels. The headline story about Japan is that the bubble economy of the 1980s was popped by central bank policy, and through bad policy choices, the country has remained mired in deflation and low growth for the entire 20-plus years since. Yet, even the casual visitor to Japan remains struck by how rich it is and how modern and comfortable daily life remains. Two points come to mind: first, a nation that has created great wealth does not become poor or lose its institutions and skills overnight; second, people adapt to their circumstances. Turning to the first, the net worth of the American household sector remains massively positive even after the massive wealth destruction of the 2008 crisis. The corporate business sector balance sheet is in rude health

The second point is more important; people do adapt to reality and cope better than expected in most cases. The Japanese bubble economy was fed by absurd equity and real estate markets, both of which remain far below their 1980s levels. For one thing, life has become more affordable for more people with steady incomes, since prices have fallen (and to a degree, still are) and housing is more affordable. Japan still runs a version of the insider-versus-outsider labor market, with the government, banks, and global export industries on the inside—but the ironclad lifetime employment of the famous Japanese "salary man" is a thing of the past. More workers, especially young workers, are no longer willing to be salary men, and more women, though not enough, are joining the work force and professions. While institutions to support entrepreneurship and start-ups are weak, there are more of them. Some of the most exciting new concepts in Japanese business are being driven by Softbank, led by the ultimate outsider: a Japanese Korean.

There are, of course, problems, but Japan has a national social solidarity and a self-discipline that are very useful under extreme stress. We saw that in the devastating earthquake and tsunami of 2011. Japanese government is highly dysfunctional, even by American standards, and corporate governance and candor sorely wanting. This doesn't seem to matter much, as the power and prestige of institutions have receded. The country could do better with more reform, but there is no sense of crisis. Instead, Japan seems to be finding its way on a long and steady path toward being the first "post-growth" society. This is partially driven by demography, an aging population, and low birth rate, which means there will be many fewer Japanese people in future. This of course means less economic growth, but also less need for it. Given the choice between maintaining their cultural homogeneity and growth through immigration, they will choose the former. In America, such a choice would be greeted with moral outrage; in Japan, it doesn't even seem a choice. On the path they are now, the Japanese can maintain a relatively high standard of living for many generations given the accumulated wealth and inventiveness of the society. The great virtue of a trust-based society with shared values is that class warfare and ethic tension don't come into play in politics and everyday life, making gentle adjustment to reduced expectations possible.

I am not for a moment suggesting that America can or should literally attempt to "go Japanese" in the sense of adopting a stoical resignation that graceful decline must be accepted. America is almost the opposite type of society in many ways. What I am suggesting is that individuals in a society can adapt to financial deleveraging and diminished growth prospects, even if the big institutions, especially government, fail to do the right thing. In other words, there is much we can learn from how Japanese society responds to institutional failure. Currently, public policy in the United States is massively self-contradictory. On one hand, the authorities seem to want to reinflate the very asset bubble that led to the crisis through ultra-loose monetary policy. On the other, they insist on beating the financial services industry into a pulp and reducing it to a public utility that dare not take risks. Americans resist basic entitlement and tax reform, and empower insider interest groups, instead of focusing on global competitiveness and entrepreneurship. The odds of any of this getting resolved politically are pretty long. We need to take matters in our own hands to the degree possible.

A Little Advice

This is not a book of investment advice, and frankly the only people who make money from such books are those who write them. The following, though, are broad suggestions for the consumer in the world after finance.

Save Money!

First, you are going to have to save enough to live on after you can no longer work. This is a lesson from Japan, where although savings are now being spent down by an aging population, they are still very substantial compared to the

United States. Given the structure of employment and inevitably higher tax burdens, savings will be tough for young people, but starting young and staying on track is essential. As a practical matter, saving at least 10 percent (and, ideally, twice that) out of current income—basically what Japanese and German people did for decades and Americans did before the bubble (the United States had an 8 percent savings rate a generation ago)—could fund a comfortable retirement. Nobody under 55 should count on unfunded pay-as-you-go pension schemes such as Social Security being anything more than a shadow of what current recipients enjoy. A means tested quasi-welfare program may be affordable, but there is a limit on what taxes future generations will pay to redeem the unfunded entitlements we have voted for ourselves.

Don't Count on the House

Second, you cannot rely, as the last two generations of Americans did, on house prices to rise. The US housing market is vastly overbuilt, and millions of "homeowners" are still in their houses without paying mortgages. This is a far more serious housing depression than even that of the 1930s, and may take decades to resolve. Housing is shelter, not a financial asset to produce future income. House price appreciation can produce a windfall if one buys and sells at the right moment and carrying costs are less than the gain, but it cannot be counted upon to build wealth. Federal and state programs to provide "relief" to homeowners not only prevent the housing market from clearing and begin rising, but also so violate basic contract rights of the lenders that the terms and supply of mortgage finance may be reduced permanently. Although it seems downright un-American, it often makes sense to rent rather than buy. Many households who own homes in communities where work has disappeared are effectively trapped by their ownership of houses that are deteriorating in value and cannot be sold.

Steer Clear of the Stock Market

Third, there is no safe way to make money in the stock market. Although they are far more liquid than real estate, equities can go down and stay down for very long periods of time. The time that one buys and sells is critical, and market timing is a very inexact and risky business. If you bought the pre-1929 Crash Dow Jones average and held it all the way through to 1960, you have done very well, at least in nominal terms. If you had to sell in 1930 or 1940, you did very badly indeed. The fabled wisdom that equities always outperform bonds over the long run is correct, but as Keynes said, in the long run we are all dead. Most of the gains in the market, and most of the losses, occur in very short inflection points that are unpredictable. Buying and holding means you won't miss the good surprises, but you won't avoid the bad ones either.

What is certain is that equities are a claim on future earnings, which are always subject to events and shifts in sentiment. Given that, companies that make money in transparent ways and can actually pay a dividend to shareholders are often safer bets. The virtues of diversification have been oversold because in a panic, assets tend to fall across the board, but investing in index funds that mirror whole markets or broadly diversified mutual funds is probably well advised for the average investor. One point to bear in mind is that the emerging markets are likely to grow much faster over the next several years and decades than the mature economies of the West. Direct investing in such markets can be risky and costly, but you can participate in their growth by investing in US companies with strong and growing footprints in those countries.

Be Wary of Bonds and Money Market Funds

Fourth, the very logic of financial repression is one of minimizing returns to the bondholders, and this will not change without a significant tightening in monetary policy. There is very little to be gained in holding government debt right now that cannot be had in a low-interest but insured bank account that is a lot more liquid. If some debt instruments offer better yields than prime corporate and government bonds, you are probably taking on a lot more risk. The Fed policy is literally forcing institutional investors to take on more and more risk in search of returns, and certain exotic structured products such as collateralized debt obligations are creeping back into the market. With the central banks flooding the market with liquidity, the market is too distorted and the yield curves too flat (long-term and short-term rates are about the same) for ordinary investors to navigate. Also, don't take for granted that money market funds are risk free in today's world.

Stay Debt Free

Fifth, not spending money is as good as earning more money in a repressed economy. For starters, if your portfolio is doing a bit better than the market, but you are paying substantial management or advisor fees, it can cancel out. Transaction costs and taxes can also dilute your returns. Beyond avoiding excess investment costs, there is a good case for simplification and even downsizing of our lives to assure that we live within our means across the board. Any lifestyle that requires the accumulation of consumer debt and does not fit into current income is unsustainable over time and extremely stressful.

This is particularly true when the odds of maintaining continuous employment and income are deteriorating due to structural changes in the global economy, not a temporary recession. Avoidance of debt is a form of freedom.

You, Inc.

Sixth, and finally, view yourself as an enterprise and invest accordingly in being economically viable by developing skills that command income in the market. The old paradigm of steady employment in large organizations that so many of our institutions, from health insurance to retirement savings, revolved around was falling apart for a generation before the crisis. Now it's shattered, and we all have to live in an economy where we justify our economic value day by day in competition with others in a networked economy. Hoping the old world of promised economic security—the world of the New Deal consensus—can be revived will not make it so. Build up your network and constantly be looking for a way to create your next opportunity.

Reconstructing Finance

Relearning and Living the Basics

Today the financial services industry in the rich world—sometimes just called "the banks"—finds itself, as Shakespeare put it, "in disgrace with fortune and men's eyes." What is remarkable is the degree to which "bankers" as a group just don't understand their disgrace and its consequences. Nor do the leaders of the industry fully comprehend the fact that they accumulated outlandish riches not through any talent or industry on their part (though many displayed both in high degree), but through pure grace. John Brooks, who wrote beautifully about such things in the *New Yorker* 50 years ago, titled his book on the golden age of Wall Street *Once in Golconda* (Harper & Row, 1969), after a fabled city in India so wealthy that a man only had to go in one gate to pass out the other side rich. Such was Wall Street in the days of Harding and Coolidge. If you left Yale or Williams and joined a Wall Street firm, it was hard not to become extremely well heeled in the decade before the Crash of 1929. If you look at the physical reality of New York City and its suburbs, the wealth generated in that decade still lives in hundreds of prewar luxury apartment buildings and thousands of faux-Tudor mansions, a pattern repeated in large cities across the country where big killings in the market were turned into big real estate. If you went to the Street with the same pedigree in 1934 or after, you might do all right. But the gate to Golconda was shut. Luxury buildings and big houses largely ceased to be built around the financial centers.

Fifty years later, Golconda was again open for business on an unprecedented scale. The details don't matter, and the story is told in my book, *Financial Market Meltdown*. But suffice it to say financial repression collapsed in the 1970s, along with the credibility of government management of the economy. This was not a matter of politicians such as Thatcher and Reagan waving a magic wand—a fairy tale often told. What happened was that events such as the two oil price shocks of 1973 and 1979 and the onset of double-digit inflation made the old Keynesian model of government fine-tuning the economy unworkable. Finance, having been tamed by the repressive regulation of 1930s and 1940s, was on the march again. All you had to do was join the parade or, more precisely, march under the right banner. Most old-line "money center" banks were not bursting at the seams to lead a financial revolution, nor were the old-line "white shoe" investment banks. Repression was managed to give them both a cozy cartel. They only embraced change when their future suddenly became insecure, and then it was mostly too late.

No, the parade into the new Golconda was led by a motley crew of outsiders who saw gold in the sheer rottenness of the old regime. These included take-no-prisoners bond houses, such as the Solomon Brothers, who were immortalized by Michael Lewis in *Liar's Poker* (Penguin, 1990). Michael Milken's junk bonds fueled Drexel Burnham and the leveraged-buyout firms that followed. The entire venture capital industry that funded Silicon Valley and much else was equally new as a market force, though it traces its roots to the repressed 1940s. Private equity represented another essentially new industry in the 1980s, and the same is true for hedge fund industry that grew up a decade or so later. Joining one of these battalions, or one of a handful of the established players, such as Goldman Sachs, that learned to play across almost all new products and markets, almost guaranteed vast rewards. Only at the turn of the 1990s did mainstream banks of the world begin to put serious resources into the new markets and instruments that had transformed finance from the outside in response to investors seeking higher returns, innovators seeking capital, and a new breed of corporate raiders seeking a killing.

A seminal moment came in 1999 when the last vestiges of Glass-Steagall were swept away, largely after they had fallen into disuse. By then the game was already changed beyond recognition, and 1930s-style regulation had become a dead letter. What had once been private partnerships became public companies so they could raise the capital to invest in trading and, as important, the technology to support trading in competition with big global banks determined to build or buy their way into the new Golconda.

As in the 1920s, life in Golconda seems natural to its inhabitants. So when it shuts its gates and rolls up its gilded streets, these things are viewed as temporary aberrations in the natural order of things. Banking and, even more, investment banking, have always been what are called "cyclical businesses," a polite term for "boom and bust." In a market economy, investors and lenders always get overconfident in good times and overshoot into bubbles followed by crises. The first instinct of market participants, who rarely have personal experience of extended downturns, since up to 2008 there had not been any since the early 1980s, is that time will solve the problem. Markets always come back. Except, of course, when they don't. The new "Masters of the Universe," as Tom Wolfe dubbed the Sherman McCoys of this world in *The Bonfire of the Vanities* (Bantam, 1998), actually believed that their way of life is natural. After the panic of 2008 recedes in memory, people will become less hostile to finance, regulations will prove unworkable, and the political tide will turn. No doubt Richard Whitney, Chairman of the New York Stock Exchange and uncrowned king of the 1920s Golconda, felt the same way, at least until he was headed to Sing Sing.

This sanguine sense of the natural order of things, rather than simple moral turpitude, explains in good measure why the banks saved from the brink of failure by unprecedented amounts of public support handed out such offensive bonuses in 2010 and 2011 (2012 compensation, while still incomprehensible to mere mortals, is shaping up to be relatively subdued). If you actually believed that the markets would bounce back, not paying generous bonus compensation was a form of unilateral disarmament. Other banks would poach away your top "producers," leaving your bank at a crucial disadvantage when the gates to Golconda again swing open. This was, after all, a cyclical business and one that depended on talent.

In 1997, McKinsey and Company, a reliable servant of the best-paid bankers and executives, coined the term "War for Talent," an idea that was picked up by other business theorists and the human resources profession as "the race for talent." The notion was that the activities of a bank or corporation depended on "talent" as much as, say, a professional sports team. Paying up for talent was part of your strategic edge, as the New York Yankees had long demonstrated. Of course, the McKinsey analysis was far subtler than this implies, but the connection between talent and highly remunerated jobs in finance would have amused the *New Yorker's* John Brooks, who described the apelike behavior of bond traders. If an activity becomes wildly overcompensated, it will obviously attract a lot of driven and capable people. In fact, the disproportionate rewards of finance arguably deflected a whole generation of selective university graduates away from other potentially more socially and culturally valuable pursuits. Whether being clever and ambitious is comparable to athletic or artistic talent, both rare commodities, is another question.

In December of 2009, long after the bubble had burst, Martin Taylor, the former CEO of Barclays Bank, wrote an opinion piece in the *Financial Times* entitled "Innumerate Bankers Were Ripe for Reckoning," suggesting that the flaw in the system of rewards that had led finance astray was simple math:

> *All business people know that you can carry on for a while if you make no profits, but if you run out of cash you are toast. Bankers, as providers of cash to others, know this well. They just do not believe it applies to them ... [in 2007] observers of financial services saw unbelievable prosperity and apparently immense value added. Yet two years later the industry was bankrupt. A simple reason underlies this: any industry that pays out in cash colossal accounting profits that are largely imaginary will go bust quickly.*

Bankers were not evil or greedy, at least not necessarily so, but they certainly couldn't count. Bank trading revenues, which might be as high as 80 percent of their pretax profits, were based on accounting calculations (a trade is profitable if the resulting position is above a "mark-to-market" price at the time) and, unlike old-fashioned lending or advisory work, generated little or no cash flow. This is why, mysteriously, so many banks can show good trading profits at the same time without producing big losers. Trading is not poker. However, as in poker, the chips won in the game can be redeemed for cash. Therefore, the management and traders of a big complex bank could take out real money in return for generating paper accounting profits that might never be realized on a cash-flow basis. The shareholders, of course, would bear the cash cost for all the "talent" and be the only ones to suffer (except perhaps the public, as in 2008) if the paper profits turned out to be fictions. As Taylor pointed out, on a cash-flow basis, any other business would fail if it paid out more in compensation that it took in. And, as we have seen, in the event of failure, the fortunes removed from the firm would remain secure in the hands of the departed "talent."

Since the all-male, White Anglo-Saxon Protestant Ivy League Golconda of the 1920s, banking had become transformed by the 1990s into a global meritocracy of highly credentialed citizens of the world representing all genders and nationalities. The openness of the system across race and gender lines was also reflected in iconic training grounds such as Harvard Business School and McKinsey. This global and diverse "talent pool" helped legitimize the notion of extraordinary rewards for those who worked their way to the top in elite institutions. And, unlike the financiers of the Jazz Age, these modern denizens of Golconda were politically correct and went to high-minded conferences in places such as Davos, Switzerland, and supported progressive causes and the arts.

It must be very difficult for them to imagine that Golconda is closed and their star has faded for a long, dark night. After all, they deserved everything they had. They had the credentials to prove it.

Earning It

The actor John Houseman, who spent much of the 1980s playing a crusty law professor on TV, filmed a series of iconic commercials for retail stock broker Smith-Barney that told America, "We make money the old-fashioned way. We earn it." In 1988, the year that Houseman passed away, Smith-Barney fell into the hands of Travelers Group, the company that financier Sandy Weill used in 1999 to take over Citibank. The deal created the ultimate financial supermarket, Citigroup. Weill did not believe in making money the old-fashioned way.

As much as bankers can deploy their vast financial resources to defend their business model politically, the spirit of the age is against them. The socialist victor in the 2012 election for president of France, François Hollande, positioned his campaign as a crusade against finance, and even the Tories in London have no sympathy for the banks or excessive pay for "talent." Nobody is fighting Wall Street's corner in the 2012 American election either. It is possible, of course, that bankers can just wait it out, that all will be forgiven when the economy turns. Far more likely, banks are going to have to change their structure and behavior—what management types call their "business model." This is not a matter of cosmetic surgery. Finance needs to undergo a fundamental reconstruction, a root-and-branch transformation, so that society can again believe they "earn it."

The reconstruction of finance that I advocate is not based on abstract principles, but on a simple calculation of rational self-interest in avoiding far worse imposed outcomes for the industry and the society it serves. To be successful, it must address a number of fundamental challenges that go far beyond finding a "new business model":

- *Legitimacy:* Why should banks be tolerated by society?
- *Utility:* How can banks deliver economic value?
- *Trust:* Why can customers rely on banks not to take advantage?
- *Prudence:* How can banks keep customer money safe?

These challenges are mutually reinforcing and somewhat overlapping, but meeting them defines the objective of a program of reconstruction. *Reconstruction* is not mere "reform," but a root-and-branch change. After the US Civil War, it denoted a program of uprooting the political and social fabric of a society based on chattel slavery and replacing it with a regime based on equality under the law. Lest we forget, Reconstruction failed because in the eyes of the conquered people of the American South, it was a set of impositions to be gotten around. Externally imposed banking reform, if carried to excess, risks similar failure. Financial firms will simply double down on their effort to roll back or evade what they feel are self-contradictory and ill-conceived strictures on their ability to make a living.

Reconstruction must be a program led by the brightest and best from within the industry itself. It must begin with the horrible truth that finance has lost all legitimacy in the eyes of the broader society it depends upon for its existence. Bemoaning the "bank bashing" of financially illiterate politicians and media will not change that. It is likely that 99 percent of the population, including the vast majority of those working in the industry, do not really understand money, banking, and credit, much less the financial markets. This will not change; finance needs to change.

Legitimacy

Walter Bagehot as usual got to the heart of the matter in *Lombard Street* when he said that a long-established bank enjoyed a "privileged opportunity" to use other people's money. That privilege, like any other, was not a right, but a grant that could be withdrawn at any time. It was based on reputation for soundness and fair dealing, not power of law, since in Bagehot's day there were essentially no laws or regulations governing banking and finance. Long-established banks had over time acquired reputations that morphed into legitimacy, much as feudal warlords morphed into legitimate rulers. Legitimacy is the opposite of arbitrary power; it is based ultimately on service to society. Kings that served only themselves and were so perceived lost legitimacy. The same is true of the Lords of Finance.

Legitimacy in finance requires a convincing answer to the question, "Why should a bank, financial institution, or market be allowed to exist by the rest of society?" This is not an idle question, given the vast destruction of wealth and employment in the real economy that arose from the Panic of 2008 and the equally vast taxpayer resources and government debt absorbed in saving the system. This is the moral equivalent of a legitimate monarch losing a major war he started. It does not help to deflect blame or point out past service to the nation. Finance can point to the Golconda years of 1982 to 2008 as an unprecedented era of growth and general prosperity worldwide that lifted a billion people out of poverty. It can also with some justice point out how bad public policy was the root of the crisis. Nobody will be moved who isn't already in the banks' corner.

Rebuilding legitimacy requires a number of things to satisfy the sense of justice most ordinary people feel in their bones. Since we can expect the state and legal systems to attack individual banks and bankers for years if not decades, the natural and legally sound posture of top bankers will be to defend their past actions and current practices. This will only put off the restoration of legitimacy. Only a candid and humble admission of their own portion of blame for the current disaster can earn banks a hearing in the prevailing atmosphere. What exactly should they confess to? Not crime, because the worst results came from what was legal or even compelled by bad policy and law. Bankers should confess to hubris, a tragic flaw, and their own arrogance and ignorance. Truth be told, financial innovations in the wholesale financial markets of the 1990s far outstripped the ability of even the most sophisticated banks to properly understand and control their risks. Their regulators, then and now, were more clueless by whole orders of magnitude.

Banks such as J. P. Morgan and Goldman did better than their hapless peers, but that owes more to good judgment by individuals such as Jamie Dimon than to the false gods of quantitative risk management. Talleyrand, speaking of his boss Napoleon's abduction and execution of the Duke of Enghien, said, "It is worse than a crime, it is a blunder." Actually, this is too cynical. Admitting that one has blundered and accepting full responsibility is the shortest path to restoring legitimacy. A measure of Robert E. Lee's greatness was riding out to greet the shattered divisions returning from Pickett's Charge with the simple message: "It is all my fault." What banker has said as much? Of course, no politician has either, but that is irrelevant. The legitimacy of banking is what is at issue.

So, what was wrong with the old banking model that needs to be confessed to as a blunder? The moment when banking or finance as a whole lost legitimacy was when the object of management became maximizing shareholder value as crudely measured by stock price. Since stock price is closely linked to return on equity—how much money a company earns on invested capital—this is an invitation to minimize capital and manipulate earnings through financial engineering. Leverage—that is, working the business with borrowed money—was always considered a grave fault in would-be borrowers by an older generation of bankers. It vastly increases the odds that some unforeseen shock will render a company unable to pay its bills. Banks also looked to borrowers to keep a cushion of capital—stock and cash preferably—as a buffer, and where possible demanded marketable collateral. It was only in the 1980s that bankers became clever enough to discard these time-honored rules, especially when applied to themselves. After the 2008 crisis, the Center for the Study of Financial Innovation in London published a very entertaining online book called *Grumpy Old Bankers*, in which bankers of an earlier era representing many countries opined on how the current generation "lost the plot" and disgraced the profession. Short-term share-price manipulation through leverage and asset securitization is high among their complaints.

The Bonus Trap

The first bank to openly abandon the "bonus culture" of compensation based upon meeting share-price targets will gain enormous moral capital and legitimacy. Even if initially recognized dimly by the general public, its peers, customers, and shareholders will take notice. As personally greedy as individuals at the top of such institutions may or may not be, the current model of compensation is a nightmare for all large banks. Employees in key market-facing roles may not be talent in the sports-star sense, but they all behave like free agents. Changing employers, often taking whole teams of expensive specialists in the process, is the road to riches. In good times, or in a hot market for a newly coined financial instrument, the current system amounts to blackmail. The talent can raise its share of bank earnings by simply threatening to switch firms. Not only is there an active army of headhunters to lubricate the process, but every employer is driving with a rearview mirror, since past performance is at least somewhat knowable, but future performance is not. How much real economic value is lost and gained by talent switching firms in unknowable, given the interplay between market conditions, sheer dumb luck, and skill. If this is true of traders and rainmakers, it is equally applicable to all executives.

In what is sometimes referred to as the "robber baron" era of capitalism, JP Morgan built a merchant bank of enormous power, consolidating entire industries, such as steel. (U.S. Steel in its heyday was the largest firm on earth.) His rule of thumb was that no professional manager was worth more than 20 times the wage of the typical employee in a firm. In the United States, and to a slightly lesser degree the United Kingdom, the ratio of top management compensation has exploded to the point that CEOs make as much as hundreds or even thousands of employees. Given how little correlation exists between payment of top management and shareholder wealth, Morgan would be appalled at today's practices. In his own bank, men who earned their way into partnership acquired a stake in the business but had to keep their capital in the business until they retired or left the firm. To take out capital, partners were required to make a personal application to Morgan himself. Old-line Wall Street partnerships, such as Goldman Sachs before it went public in 1999, were essentially the same, as were professional services firms such as McKinsey and "white shoe" law firms.

Would the "talent" stand for abandoning the bonus culture and stock-based compensation? Even absent the looming threat of government pay policies in the United Kingdom and elsewhere, there is wide recognition that the current model cannot be sustained. The brutal fact of the matter is that good-quality professional management training—from formal settings such as MBA schools to apprenticeships in analyst programs at consulting firms and investment banks—has never been as widely available as it is today. In Morgan's day, perhaps 2 percent of adult males possessed college credentials, something that was by the early 20th century becoming expected in management candidates, and MBAs numbered in the dozens of degrees granted per year. The credentialed talent pool was very small, which is why it was still possible to work one's way up to top management from the proverbial shop floor.

Today there are at least hundreds if not thousands of men and women of all nationalities with formal credentials comparable to each of the highest-paid incumbents in finance and public companies generally. In other words, talent is anything but a scarce commodity. If it is massively overpriced, this represents institutional governance flaws, especially the so-called agency problem. Boards too often do not effectively represent shareholder interest, but are creatures of the professional management of the firm. Pay practices, legitimized by a specialized executive compensation consulting industry, reflect this and can charitably be called a market failure. Large public companies are more like feudal kingdoms than embodiments of market capitalism.

Oddly, although market capitalism is under siege in the political world—see the *Financial Times* series "Capitalism in Crisis" for a range of views—large financial institutions and public companies have never fully embraced its rigors. In finance, legitimacy means walking the talk on market capitalism. Talent will bifurcate—and indeed already has—into those willing to risk their own capital and those content to play with other people's money. The former are already flocking to the private equity and especially the hedge fund world. There, rewards are infinite in theory, but there is no government safety net. In a rough-and-ready way, this is fair as long as only "sophisticated investors," as defined by reasonable regulators, are at risk. In general, these industries probably have seen their best days, as witnessed by pioneers such as KKR cashing out by going public. And politicians do love to hate them, except when raising funds, so the tax and regulatory paradise that made them so lucrative cannot last unscathed. However, this so-called shadow banking system is as close to real market capitalism as it gets, at least since the Victorian standard of merchant banks being private partnerships with unlimited liability. Whatever its flaws, as long as the principals in the business have their own fortunes at risk, making bets on the future is a legitimate activity and a socially useful one. Without gamblers and speculators, there would be no liquid markets in equity and debt, but above all there would be no seed money for innovation in technology and business—perhaps the single most distinctive advantage of the American economy.

The talent that does not want to hazard the high seas of market capitalism can, like the generations of finance professionals between 1933 and 1982, embrace essentially bureaucratic careers administering sober, socially useful public institutions entrusted with other people's money. There is no shortage of very capable men and women who would make such a choice.

Utility

The banking system of any country performs a series of mundane and not-well-understood but vital functions. These are often called *financial intermediation*: taking in deposits from people who have surplus money and investing it in securities and loans to people in need of money. In theory—and we do see a few Internet-based direct-lending models emerging that may make the theory workable—providers and users of money should be able to find each other, but beyond a household, a circle of friends, or a village, this is impractical. Financial middlemen and markets solve really big information and risk challenges for both sides. For centuries this has been the key "utility function" of proper banks. Given the mismatch at any given time between when depositors want their money and when borrowers need funds, banks also in effect create money in this process. Without functioning financial intermediaries, people cannot borrow today to create more income—what is sometimes called working capital—tomorrow. Bank credit therefore sustains and grows economic activity and employment.

The second utility function of banks is the transmission of economic value over time and space. Historically, this was accomplished through the most basic and protean of financial instruments, the bill of exchange. As early as the 12th century, merchants were paying distant providers of goods with negotiable IOUs that could be discounted for cash locally or used as a form of currency. When something resembling modern banks came into existence in trading centers such as Venice, Genoa, Amsterdam, and London during the 16th and 17th centuries, they learned by trial and error that it was economical to net out the value of bills that customers had drawn on each other for a small cash settlement. This was the origin of the clearinghouse.

These institutions came in two basic flavors. The first obliged all players in the bills-of-exchange market to keep an account in a single public bank, such as the Banco di Giro in Venice. When bills became due—all bills of exchange instructed payment of a specific sum at a specific date to whomever held the bill—the bank owing the money transferred it to the account of the bank due the funds. The "giro" payments systems of Central and Northern Europe all emerged from these practices. In London, by contrast, a second flavor took hold. The private banks there did not use a single public bank, because the only public bank was the Bank of England, their arch-competitor. So instead, all the other private banks swapped bills on each other in a clearinghouse (originally a tavern), which excluded the Bank of England, and settled up in cash. All the payments systems in the English-speaking world are basically extensions of this mechanism. From these simple pragmatic arrangements, something known as the payments system was born, but after four centuries it still revolves around the clearing and settlement of claims between banks in some type of clearinghouse.

The exchange of claims—once paper bills and checks (a stripped-down form of a bill), or transfer instructions—is called *clearing*. Settlement is simply final payment—once in specie (gold or silver) and now in central bank money—of the net sums due after clearing is completed. Your salary, bill payments, and credit and debit card transactions, and all the buying and selling between firms that make the wheels of commerce turn, ultimately flow into and out of various clearinghouses and are settled in central bank money. Making this happen in a safe, convenient, and reliable way is very complicated and very expensive in practice. Few people have a working knowledge of the detail. However, without a properly functioning payments system, any modern economy would seize up and die.

Central banks and regulators understand this very well. Since in a fiat money system there is no specie—gold and silver have been demonetized—only claims on banks, so-called deposit money, are used to store and transfer economic value in society. The protection of banks from non-bank competition, prudential regulation of their activity, the provision of central bank credit in times of stress, and, in the worst case, outright bailouts, are all features of public policy that ultimately go back to the need to protect the payments system from disruption. When people, including politicians who should know better, seek to "punish the banks," they fail to properly understand that in a modern society deposit money in the banking system accounts for almost all the ready money that households and businesses hold and use in their economic lives. For better or worse, although other entities can provide credit or places to stash your savings, only banks can effect payments.

Oddly enough, banks have over the last generation managed to turn this tremendous source of public utility into a major source of public annoyance. Before the 1980s, banks understood that payments were the key to their competitive advantage as deposit-takers. As noted previously, banking largely depends on the "privileged opportunity" of using other people's money. In an age of financial repression, especially, it is hard to compete for the public's surplus money by offering higher interest. The success of the mutual fund industry is proof that money has many places to go besides banks. Even when banks can compete by paying competitive interest on deposits, it can squeeze their margins—the difference between what they pay for money and what they charge for it—severely. Payments are a way for compensating depositors for the use of their money in kind rather than in cash. The deal, at least implicitly, used to be, "Give us your money for free or close to free, and we will make and receive payments for you."

Economists use the term "liquidity premium" for the preference for transferable money over less liquid investments. In theory, money should seek the highest rate of return, but in any banking system people keep liquid funds at levels well above their day-to-day requirements. This is in large measure a function of the payment utility provided by banks. There is strong positive correlation between the use of payment services by bank customers and their deposits in demand or current accounts, as well as linked savings accounts. In fact, in the pre-crisis interest rate environment, this liquidity-premium effect drove half or more of banks profits. If you factor in payment-related credit provisions such as current account overdrafts or revolving credit card balances, the liquidity premium could exceed two-thirds of earnings for some banks. Customers simply accepted the fact that they would receive below-market interest on deposits and pay above-market interest on loans related to payment transactions. This helps to explain why banks put so much effort into expanding the "banked" population in the 1960s and 1970s—transaction accounts were very profitable. Giving away toasters for opening them was a good use of money if the result was the ownership of checking accounts becoming almost universal among the employed population.

Then, banks again lost the plot. The old integrated model of lending other people's money safely and paying for it with deposit and payment services was simple. It was also dull and mechanical, more like a public utility than a growth industry. In the 1980s, two things happened to undermine this cozy, regulated franchise. One was simply that the banks' best and most natural loan customers, large corporations, found it cheaper to borrow money in the public markets. The second was that the same public capital markets, led by the institutions that managed retirement savings, began to demand higher returns on their investments and growth in earnings. On top of that, the largest banks had as a herd charged into one growth area after another—the worst being loans to foreign governments—to solve both these problems. These bets were rewarded with vast losses and banks were forced to embark upon an urgent rethinking of their basic business model.

For better or worse, much of this rethinking was done by McKinsey, especially its banking-practice led by Lowell Bryan. McKinsey as a firm had grown up with American industry and its postwar organizational challenges, expanding its consulting business globally on the basis of this experience. It came to financial services late, but with great focus and talent. Quickly the firm established itself as the go-to guys for the struggling banking industry of the 1980s. Dated as they are, Bryan's two seminal books of the period, *Breaking up the Bank* (Irwin Professional, 1988) and *Bankrupt* (HarperCollins, 1992), provide insight into the advice that McKinsey was providing to leading banks in the US and beyond. Bryan forcefully and correctly analyzed why the traditional banking business model was unviable in the face of growing competition from the capital markets. The firm's prescriptions were often less sound than its diagnoses. McKinsey, perhaps unconsciously, found itself urging the financial services industry to adopt the same kinds of organization, business models, and strategies it had developed through long and deep experience in manufacturing and retailing. Banks, grown dull by their long existence as cozy regulated utilities, were in need of fresh thinking to be sure. However, in practice McKinsey (and other consultancies that imitated it) educated banks in the arts of organizing and optimizing discrete product businesses competing in defined product markets, as if they were conventional industrial enterprises rather financial intermediaries. Banks, which had formerly been remarkably integrated and simple businesses, became increasingly fragmented into complex matrices of product business "silos," each with its own profit and growth objectives, strategies and resource demands.

When I first became a banker in 1974, the word *product* was virtually never used, nor was there a "product management discipline" or "product silos." There were line divisions organized by geography: metropolitan, national, and international. There was an operations division that managed accounts and inbound and outbound payments. Above all, there was credit, which evaluated all lending. By 1994, banks were engaged in manufacturing products, distributing them through sales channels, and managing vastly complex and expensive technology infrastructures to support both. The truth of the matter was that the whole division of "originating," "packaging," and "distributing" credit that lay at the heart of the 2008 panic was an outgrowth of this industrial model of banking.

There was undoubted value in breaking up the old integrated model of banking, where measurement and accountability were weak, into accountable "profit centers," where managers had to "make their numbers" or perish. McKinsey had half a century of deploying this multidivisional, or "M-form," organization of devolved responsibility in manufacturing. (Duff McDonald's upcoming book on McKinsey, *The Professionals*, points out how important this concept, perfected if not originated by Alfred Sloan at GM, was to the firm's success.) The problem was that, strictly speaking, banks have no products. They simply have accounts opened by customers, which they operate on the customer's behalf. They are what Dickens called "counting houses" and at heart could be run on a spreadsheet. All their activity consists of moving instructions to debit and credit accounts to and from that spreadsheet. As Bagehot famously put it, "Banking is a simple business, the simplest that could be imagined." The re-imagined banking of the 1980s and 1990s became extremely complicated.

First, there was a multiplication of products, each with its own management, infrastructure, and strategy. Many of these, such as credit cards and home equity loans, were novel ways to originate consumer credit. Second, there were new distribution channels, such as ATMs, direct mail, call centers, and of course home computers. Eventually, the Internet, mobile telephones, and social media joined the mix. Third, there was a multiplication of specialized software and networks to support these products. Bank systems grew in cost and complexity as IT became a bigger share of banks' budgets, as did product development and marketing—all things banks spent very little on before the 1980s. On top of all this, banks' basic cost structure and systems continued to revolve around so-called core banking: posting the credit and debits to accounts, processing payments, and otherwise keeping the counting house in balance. "Brick-and-mortar" distribution costs—the real estate and people involved in a branch network—were targets of the new technological distribution systems, but never went away. Customers, especially consumers, simply could not be made to use only the cost-effective channels banks wanted them to use.

There was only one way to make such a complex and costly banking model pay. That was to press every product silo to increase its bottom line by any means possible. On the cost side, banks' ability to properly understand, much less hold down, their costs was about as good as Congress's attempts at spending restraint. Core costs, just like the entitlement programs in the government budget, were the largest share of bank budgets, and were driven by nondiscretionary factors, such as software maintenance and regulatory compliance, that more or less put the budgets on autopilot. Real estate footprints could be cut back, but at competitive risk. Periodic headcount reductions— a McKinsey specialty called OVA, for "overhead value analysis"—provided short-term relief. So did outsourcing functions in technology and customer services to low-cost areas and countries such as South Dakota and India. However, cost and complexity grew relentlessly, especially after banks began to merge into regional and national giants. Many mergers were advertised as creating economies of scale like those in manufacturing, but diseconomies of scale were more typical in banking. The cost of complexity overwhelmed what scale and scope advantages were achievable.

So, the pressure on managers in the lines of business organized around products fell overwhelmingly on the revenue side. It is hard to generate more demand for credit among creditworthy borrowers, so as we have seen time and again in banking's roller-coaster history, lenders began to inch further and further out on the risk curve. Loan losses and regulatory oversight set some limits to what could be done with lending, however, especially as competition and market-based substitutes held down margins overall. Banks found, again with the help of McKinsey and other consultants, an almost limitless ability to create and grow fee revenue, usually referred to as "non-interest income."

Between the early 1980s and the period just before the crisis, banks in the United States more than doubled their non-interest income from around 20 percent of revenues to over 40 percent. Some of this reflected trading and advisory revenue in large banks, but the lion's share was related to deposit accounts and payments, as detailed in a fascinating Federal Reserve Bank of Chicago paper by economists Robert DeYoung and Tara Rice called "How Do Banks Make Money?" (*Economic Perspectives*, Q4 2004). For the whole period from 1970 to 2003, net interest income, the basic intermediation utility, fell from over 80 percent of bank revenues to less than 60 percent in the United States. Fees moved from well below 20 percent to above 40 percent in the same period. In fact, fee-income growth has been the leading driver of retail bank profitability for a generation. In the process, banks have come to depend on fee revenue from households to a dangerous extent. As noted in Chapter 3, the government has effectively gained the ability to cap and roll back these fees in the wake of the crisis, as demonstrated by the industry backing down in the face of consumer and political pressure over debit card fees in late 2011.

In principle, price fixing by government is economically damaging and to be avoided. Banks, however, pressed the science of maximizing fees so far that the sheer utility value of banks fell out of balance with public perceptions of basic fairness and value for money. This was not an evil plot by bank executives, but a natural consequence of running scores of uncoordinated product silos "by the numbers" with no overall comprehension of the contribution a household was making to bank income and expense. Creative approaches to generating more bounced checks and unintentional overdrafts through manipulating the timing of posting credits and debits to customer accounts is a case in point. A very successful consultancy was constructed around this practice, which fell most heavily on the lowest-income customers of banks. The product managers were not being consciously cruel and duplicitous. They were trying to keep their jobs.

Technology to the Rescue

The reconstruction of banking will depend on increasing utility while decreasing costs, something that has happened in almost every corner of the economy except banking and services delivered by or funded by government, such as education and health care. Information technology has already made vast productivity gains in banking, essentially by converting paper-based information logistics to electronic processes. However, to a remarkable degree, the introduction of information technology into banking was a matter of "paving the cow path." The clerical routine and customary practices of banking, often at the level of individual banks, was replicated by bank software applications. Things became "better, faster, cheaper" when transactions became electronic. They did not become fundamentally different. And in many areas, especially the payments system, large amounts of paper persisted and still persist. Cash, essentially government-issued notes and coin, still accounts for about 9 out of 10 retail transactions worldwide. Since it circulates hand to hand outside of the banking system, cash usage can only be estimated. To a very large extent, bank branches exist to allow cash deposits by retailers and small businesses, functions that tie them to a specific bank. While less cash is drawn over bank counters, cashing checks is a major requirement for many consumers and businesses. Checks themselves have been resilient in the face of decades of bank investment to replace them.

Anglo-Saxon-type banking systems still have billions of check payments, as does France. Cash and checks are in decline, largely as a by-product of payment cards and electronic bank-to-bank transfers. However, nobody seriously predicts their elimination in the foreseeable future, because they still have utility to payers and payees in a wide range of circumstances. Otherwise, they wouldn't be used. From a bank perspective, in check-writing countries such as the United States (which accounts for the vast majority of all checks), no product generates a higher liquidity premium or more fee revenue per account. Clearing checks is the most profitable activity of the Federal Reserve System and a big moneymaker for correspondent banks. As for cash, central banks basically print the stuff for pennies per note and sell it to banks at face value. This currency monopoly of the state is called seigniorage and is worth tens of billions to governments around the world. All these things leave banks and even central banks conflicted about how much effort they should invest in trying to force the remaining paper out of the system. In part, this lack of investment commitment reflects the fact many cash services like ATMs can defend their stand-alone profitability, but the main inhibitor is that branch networks, ATMs, and physical-paper-handling logistics cannot be eliminated substantially unless cash and checks fall out of use almost entirely. No one bank, no matter how big, can change the game by withdrawing from paper payments without losing customers to banks that still provide these services.

Of course, bank customers once routinely used gold and silver coin in everyday life, along with the bank notes and checks that replaced them, so things can change. A new generation reared on mobile phones and the Internet is unlikely to persist in the use of paper in financial transactions. However, given prolonged financial repression, banks will need to make massive reductions in their cost structures to meet constricted revenue opportunities and vastly increased regulatory and litigation expense. Anything less than a 50 percent takedown will most likely prove inadequate to maintain an adequate return on capital. The stately pace of "paper-to-electronic" migration that marked the last 50 years of bank automation is just not good enough.

The good news is that the reconstruction of finance through information technology is in fact taking place, but largely outside of the banks themselves. As long as banks are locked in a product-business construct and run key functions in their cost base—such as payments—as standalone businesses, they will fail. To cite just one example, modern web-based technology, cloud computing, and mobile telephony have upended "old media" such as TV, movies, and publishing within a decade. None of the key innovations in technology and business models originated in old media, and few old-media companies have learned to leverage them. The same is likely to happen to the banks given their structure and business culture.

To take payments as an example, almost every innovation of the last two decades (e.g., debit cards and home banking) was expected to pay for itself as a stand-alone product and was priced accordingly. This approach ignored the fact that these innovations were massively more cost effective than the channels and payment methods they displaced. An integrated view of bank income and expense, such as the one prevailing before 1980, would have viewed these innovations as ways to lower the costs of providing the branch and payment services required to gather deposits, not as a source of revenues. If electronic payments had been made essentially free or very cheap for end users, the amount of paper in the system would be far less daunting and the associated infrastructures and headcount rationalized long ago. Instead, costly paper payments, especially cash, have remained underpriced relative to electronic alternatives and so continue to be overused. Now it may be too late in the day for banks to collectively attack the remaining paper in the system given the material technology investments required. The post-crisis regulatory backlash guarantees that industry will in the coming years have far lower earnings out of which to make those investments. However, there are some steps individual banks can and should take.

First, banks must grossly simplify their offerings to their customers, the vast majority of whom have very simple financial needs. Complexity, product innovation, and product marketing are all luxuries in a world of financial repression. Bank costs must be driven down by ruthless pruning of redundant activities and better use of scarce resources. The tools of "big data" increasingly allow firms to distinguish patterns in customer behavior and identify the things that specific target customers actually use to make decisions to buy or not buy.

Second, banks should be flexible contractor/subcontractor relationships objectively managed. It does not matter if this involves outsourcing or joint ventures, and it doesn't matter how internal functions interact. Modern information technology allows firms to enter into dynamic market contracting with each other, given the vast expansion in the ability to communicate cheaply within and across organizations. Breaking the "command-and-control" mindset of these most bureaucratic of businesses will be hard, but nothing else will generate the necessary continuous cost reduction culture needed for survival.

Third, banks need to totally change how they think about transactions and instruments from the paper age. Putting a quill pen–era practice into an app is no longer good enough. For example, credit used to be based on the discounting of individual bills of exchange based on the likelihood of payment by the maker of the bill. Paper-based information logistics—that is, snail mail (in an era of sailing ships, snails were slow indeed) and quill pens—made this impractical as economic activity and credit grew rapidly in the 19th century. Bankers began lending against balance sheets and collateral simply because the old "real-bills-banking" system was too labor intensive in a paper-based world. Today, the ability to see, evaluate, and discount trade receivables using information technology already exists. However, it is being used in new credit models such as that of the New Orleans–based Receivables Exchange, but not in commercial banks.

Another area ripe for change is the 1,000-year-old practice of using correspondent banks to access national payments systems for cross-border transactions. Existing technology could easily create a clearinghouse of clearinghouses on a global, multicurrency basis. In fact, telco operators have long established that level of interoperability, something that allows global mobile and Internet communications. At the end of the day, a network is a network, and a clearinghouse is a clearinghouse. All financial transactions share a few simple elements, and one global network and one clearinghouse is within practical possibility. The cost impact would be material, as would the savings in idle cash liquidity, if banks could collapse dozens of product-specific networks into a single clearing and settlement utility. However, no incumbent bank can make this happen alone, and none is willing to abandon the product-business construct. It is unlikely that banks will move to change their business model until it is too late.

A very wise Japanese central bank veteran, Takayoshi Hatayama, has envisioned a world in which banks melt away slowly until they are little more than highly regulated deposit-takers and providers of net settlement for an essentially new financial ecology created by technology companies, mobile operators, specialist payments companies (think PayPal and Western Union), electronic money schemes, and non-bank financiers and investment vehicles. This would indeed amount to the reconstruction of finance.

Trust

In *Financial Market Meltdown*, I explain how a bank account has always been a one-sided contract in which the bank knows a lot about what the depositor is doing with his or her money, but the depositor has no clue about what the bank is doing with it. This is called information asymmetry and is a key source of profit for financial services companies. Financial firms always know a great deal more about market conditions, especially the price of money, than their customers. However, post-crisis, they have to regain the trust they have forfeited. This will require them to become much more—at the risk of using a hackneyed term—transparent. This is not just a matter of improving disclosure of contractual terms—so-called plain-English documents and the like. The masses of people, as I have said, have no real understanding of the basic workings of even the simplest financial products. The same is true of electricity. We just assume the light goes on when we flip the switch and suspect that we are paying too much. Given the degree of incomprehension of money and banking within the banks themselves, financial education is about as likely to be effective as electricity education.

Trust in banking and finance is a matter of customers with simple needs not being oversold or "up-sold" products that are too complex and dangerous for their needs or their peace of mind. In the United Kingdom, this practice, which is almost inevitable in a product-centric, "industrial" model of banking, is called "mis-selling." Examples abound, from credit insurance to subprime mortgages to prepaid cards to many forms of revolving credit, but one feature stands out. When banks, brokers, or financial advisors are incented by or reward staff with commissions, they set up what is almost always a conflict of interest in their staff between increasing their income and keeping their jobs on one hand, and the best interests of their clients on the other. The Financial Services Authority (FSA) in the United Kingdom tackled this directly in its Retail Distribution Panel. Sir Callum McCarthy, then still at the FSA, once remarked to me at an Institute of International Finance event in Washington that his work there made him wonder why banks would put their reputations for trustworthiness at risk for the fleeting gains of pushing unsuitable pension products.

The answer is simple. The product business model and mindset almost guarantees such behavior. My former partner and founder of the CBM Group, Andre Cappon, has performed rigorous quantitative analyses of sales force effectiveness in retail stock broking, financial advisory businesses, and insurance in many markets around the world. A key finding is that the most productive sales representatives in finance are the most indifferent to customer circumstances and needs, as well as product "suitability," such as a customer's ability to afford an adjustable mortgage. They focus on two things: what is easiest to sell and what produces the highest commission for them. The top producers know how to close the sale on one product—for example, a variable annuity—and will try to sell it to anybody they can get to meet with them, suitability be damned.

This is not to say that good, customer-focused financial advice doesn't exist, especially among independent professionals. The norm in large financial conglomerates has to be push products or be gone by the logic of their business model. As recently as the 1970s, every UK bank customer had at least some access to a bank manager who, at least in theory, was trying to provide sound advice and keep him or her out of financial trouble. When I was a banker in London, I had a great bank manager at Coutts, admittedly an upscale bank. He would actually call me when he noticed I had too much cash that wasn't earning interest and offer me a better deal. Today, except for elite private banks, this customer-first ethos is almost extinct. The restoration of trust will require a return to a commitment to helping customers optimize their financial resources rather than sell them "products." Large firms already enjoy a range of services from their banks called "cash management," which allow corporate treasurers to minimize their need for working capital and maximize their return on investable cash. Given the state of technology, there is no reason in principle why every household and small business could not enjoy a stripped-down version of this service.

Of course, like cash management for big companies, a household cash-management and wealth-building service would have to be paid for explicitly. This would be a revolution in bank pricing and charging philosophy. Banks suffer low trust because people, especially low-income people, sense that if they open an account with a bank, they will be hit with a raft of hidden fees and charges they don't understand fully. As noted previously, there is some reason for this view: insufficient-funds charges are triggered by posting order as well as customer behavior. Affluent customers, which banks all court, for perfectly rational reasons, usually keep enough in the bank to avoid fees or can get them waived.

This is not true for the vast middle and working classes, who are most inclined to find banking untrustworthy. Interestingly, non-bank financial services providers such as Western Union, and even check-cashers and payday-lenders, enjoy better customer acceptance of their fees because they are simple, explicit, and based on something the customer consciously wanted to do. The simple fact of the matter is that high prices are not an outrage when we know in advance what to expect and consciously decide to pay anyway. If we order a $25 glass of wine off a printed restaurant list, though the whole bottle costs half as much at retail, we don't really mind if we really want it. If a waiter suggests a glass of the house white and the bill comes in at $25, we might feel a lot differently. People accept overall that banks have to recover their costs. They are really sensitive not so much to paying for a service, but what service and how charged. This is why bank attempts to impose fees for debit cards blew up in the face of the US banks. People resented paying for access to their own money, the same reason ATM fees are unpopular. Banks will not restore trust until they develop simple, comprehensible, no-surprise tariffs for their services from which customers can explicitly pick and choose or buy as a package.

Prudence

The maestro of the Great Moderation, Federal Reserve Board Chairman Alan Greenspan, has fallen from his pedestal but remains admirably true to his faith in market capitalism. His greatest error of judgment might have been his assumption that bankers were prudent people who understood the risks they were taking with other people's money. Writing in the *Financial Times* on January 26, 2012, he says, "I was particularly distressed by the extent to which bankers, previously pillars of capitalist prudence, had allowed their equity buffers to dwindle dangerously as the financial crisis approached. Regulatory capital needs to be increased." This misses two important points. First, the rewards system of banking was based almost entirely on returns on equity, so less capital meant higher stock prices and higher bonuses. If bankers had been rewarded based on return on assets—that is, the loans and investments they made—they would have behaved differently. But they were not so compensated before the crisis, and nothing has changed in that regard. You would think a highly intelligent disciple of Ayn Rand would have noticed that individuals respond to the incentives they are given. Second, nobody in the major banks or the central banks themselves actually believed a crisis was approaching. If they had, it would not have happened. People in positions of authority thought risk management had been much improved and risk assets were not overly concentrated. Financial panics never occur in response to foreseen events. That said, regulatory capital will be increased. The real question is will we ever again have prudent bankers?

Prudence is a virtue, and like all virtues it withers under the dead hand of law and regulation. Before deposit insurance, and in a few cases after, banks used to compete for customers on the basis of how much capital they held. Edmund Safra, a wise old Levantine banker, ran his banks on that basis. Walter Bagehot lived in a world where most privately owned banks were partnerships with unlimited liability. With their personal fortunes on the line, prudence was both a virtue and a necessity. Banks made high levels of capital a basis of competition for customer deposits. In the investment world, there is a legal standard, established in an 1830 case (*Harvard vs. Amory*), called the "prudent man" rule. It essentially sets a standard of care for fiduciaries and agents that they act like any prudent man would handling his own money. This freely admits, as the Massachusetts court put it, that "the capital is always at risk." There are no sure things in finance. The point is that the prudent man limits his risks as best he can in an uncertain world.

There is probably no harsher indictment of the financial industry before the crisis than that many senior bankers came to think of formal regulation and compliance with it as a substitute for prudence. As I noted, non-banks have every right to play anywhere they want on the risk curve if only their own capital and that of sophisticated investors is as risk. Leaving aside how sophisticated pension plans and charitable endowments really are, consenting adults are perfectly entitled to take on more risk for more potential return. The fiduciary duty of a deposit-taker to the general public is a different matter entirely.

Just boosting capital buffers is not enough, and intrusive regulation tends to crush the small banks that tend to be prudent by nature. The leading banks need to get ahead of the curve rather than fight a rear-guard action. The lower-cost, narrower, simpler, more transparent business model suggested in the previous section would make it possible for deposit-takers to limit their risk-taking and still make moderate but consistent returns. Basic financial intermediation and transaction services are probably all a bank should undertake with other people's money, though this is not an iron rule. Obviously, banks need to fund themselves and hedge their exposures and those of their clients, but this does not require endless financial innovation and flogging unproven instruments.

Finally, bank managements and boards should seriously consider if the degree of concentration of the industry that has been brought about by a generation of aggressive mergers and accelerated by the crisis has created institutions that simply cannot be prudently and effectively managed. Today, 52 %

of all bank assets are concentrated in just five banks. All but one or two of which almost certainly would have failed without unprecedented infusions of government support. *The Federal Reserve Bank of Dallas 2011 Annual Report* (published in March 2012) contains an essay titled "Choosing the Road to Prosperity" which points out that during the 2008 crisis, TBTF (too big to fail) as a policy "did not exist explicitly, in law or policy—and the term itself disguised the fact that commercial banks holding roughly one-third of assets in the banking system *did essentially fail*, surviving only with extraordinary government assistance." Obviously, the managements of these megabanks believe them to be powerful earnings generators under normal economic conditions and have on the whole accepted far more onerous regulation as the price for keeping them intact. The question a prudent man or woman would ponder though is whether or not shareholders of these banks and the economy as a whole would be better served by breaking up these leviathans through voluntary market transactions and into more manageable, focused, and nimble firms.

Restoration of Values and Reputation

I have spent a great deal of my life in and around banks. Banking has always had its critics, but unlike stock brokering or insurance sales, banking was always regarded as a profession, not just a business. Professional is an overused term today, but when it meant something a couple of generations back, bankers were consciously pursuing a real profession with real standards of practice. In the community at large, they stood just a cut below lawyers and a cut above business executives. A profession is defined by values, ultimately a service ethos. That is why the term was traditionally confined to the church, the armed forces, the law, and medicine. The service ethos has perhaps weakened across the board in modern society, but nowhere more than in banking, although many honorable men and women uphold high professional standards. The reconstruction of finance and banking cannot succeed without a rediscovery of the core professional values of trust, prudence, and utility to the broader community. The institutions that accomplish this soonest will gain reputational capital, not just financial capital, upon which to rebuild their fortunes.

Index

CPSIA information can be obtained at www.ICGtesting.com
Printed in the USA
LVOW132157081012

302060LV00007B/59/P